abbott miller: design and content

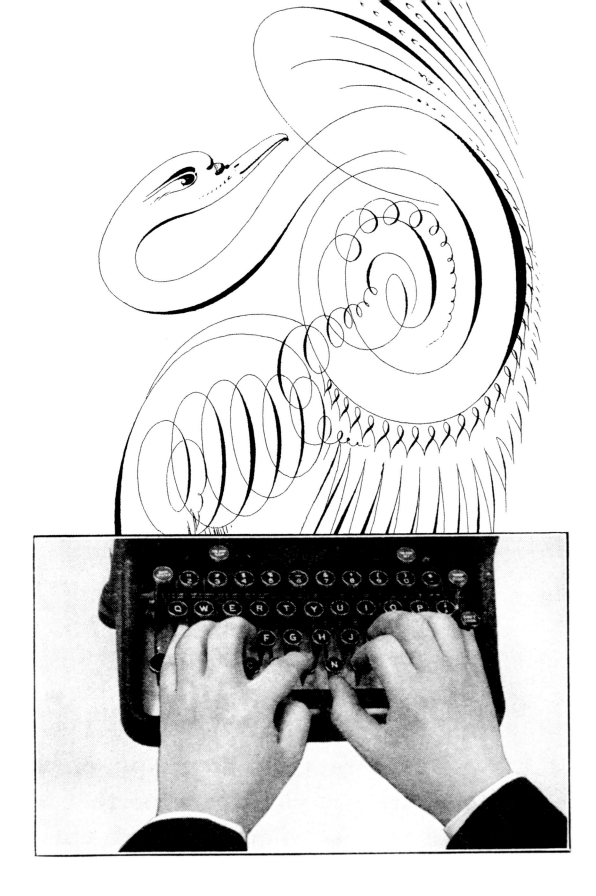

abbott miller: design and content

foreword
rick poynor

essays
ellen lupton
abbott miller

conversation
michael bierut
abbott miller
eddie opara
paula scher

PRINCETON ARCHITECTURAL PRESS, NEW YORK

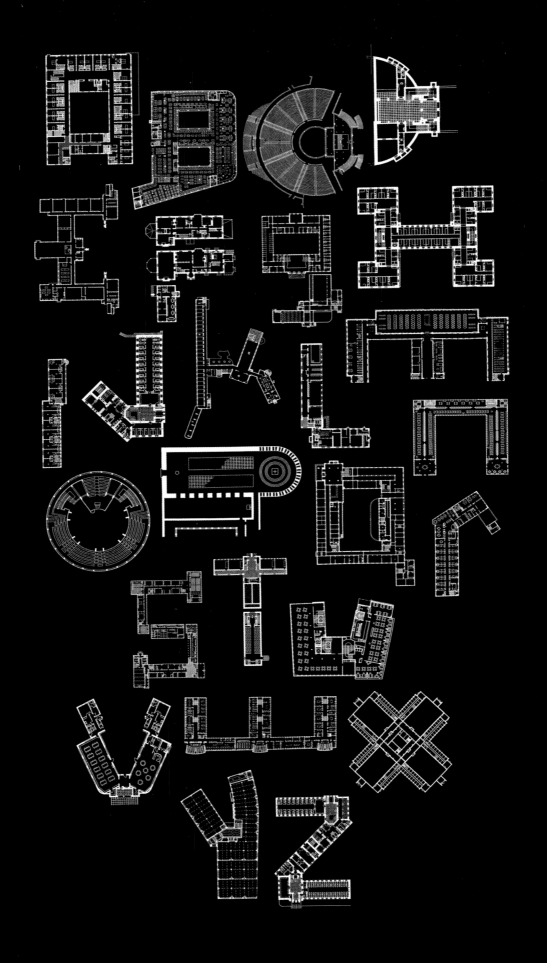

foreword

RICK POYNOR

It's funny how the origins of an innovation can become obscured, especially when a novel idea or manner of working is so successful that it creates a new norm, taken for granted by later generations who don't know where it came from or how startling it seemed at the outset. Even if you were there at the time and saw how everything unfolded, the later diffusion begins to blur the issue.

So let's set the record straight. In the early nineties, Abbott Miller and his partner Ellen Lupton—soon to be his wife—were a phenomenon, and there was no one else in American graphic design quite like them. They were a double act then, cofounders of the endeavor Design Writing Research, although their working paths would later diverge. The DWR calling card, as provocative as it was economical, galvanized the attention of anyone in graphic design who believed that the discipline could play a crucial part in excavating and interpreting a subject, as well as giving it form. Graphic design was steadily moving in this direction as a self-proclaimed means of authorship, and there were plenty of historical precedents. But Lupton and Miller's concentration and confidence, their unabashedly cerebral demeanor and presentational poise—they were still in their twenties—was unusual and impressive. They followed up the exhibition and catalogue *The ABC's of ▲■●: The Bauhaus and Design Theory* (1991) with the even more conceptually and visually daring *The Bathroom, the Kitchen, and the Aesthetics of Waste: A Process of Elimination* (1992). They both started PhD programs and then gave them up; they didn't seem to need them.

In 1996, their book *Design Writing Research: Writing on Graphic Design* confirmed their lasting significance in the recent history of graphic design and design writing. Since then, many designers in the United States, Europe, and around the world have emerged with similar aspirations to combine design with writing, publishing, and curating, though few have met the standard for total authorship set by Lupton and Miller.

During this period, I was editing *Eye* and Miller wrote several essays for the magazine, including a timely reevaluation of stock photography; a profile of Quentin Fiore that helped redirect attention to his book designs for Marshall McLuhan; and a prophetic, pathfinding piece titled "The Idea is the Machine." I valued him highly as a contributor. In 1997, I visited the DWR studio and was amazed to find that it was possible, at least in Manhattan, to maintain a venture on this scale, despite a not-very-commercial focus on exhibitions and editorial work. By this time, Miller was deep into his collaboration with Patricia Tarr on the magazines *Dance Ink* and then *2wice*, for which he asked me to write several essays. It seemed like he had, in his mid thirties, achieved a working freedom that would leave other intellectually inclined graphic designers openmouthed with envy. It came as a surprise to learn, a year or so later on another visit to New York, that Miller had been approached by Pentagram and he was seriously considering becoming a partner.

I have nothing against Pentagram yet this was still troubling news. No matter how cleverly organized or cultured Pentagram might be, it is located at the heart of the design establishment. At the point when Miller appeared to have everything going his own way as a brilliant independent, he was contemplating rebuilding his practice on much more conventional, and potentially far less fertile, terrain. I remember sounding a note of caution. He spent a year thinking about the decision and concluded there was more to gain than to lose. All the evidence collected in this volume suggests that he was right. He was able to bring existing clients with him and continue working in the same editorially and curatorially inclined fashion, yet on a bigger canvas. He has gained immeasurably from the support of experienced colleagues, and he has continued to grow as an idea-driven designer of great graphic refinement. He radiates the impression—this is surely the clincher—that from the security of this design stronghold, there is a lot more content to come.

2wice: How to Pass, Kick, Fall, and Run, 2007.
Photograph by Jens Umbach

Page 2: Collage for a *New York Review of Books*, 2009

Page 4: *Architectural Alphabet*, 2004

mr. abbott miller twice removed Abbott Miller presents Abbott Miller's work in a presentation about how books become environmental and how environments become editorial. Abbott has described Miller as a designer who thinks like an editor, and an editor who works like a designer. Wednesday, February 11, 2004, 6:30 pm, Tishman Auditorium, Parson's School of Design / New School University, 66 West 12th Street, New York

design and content

ABBOTT MILLER

George Bernard Shaw reportedly once said that the United States and Great Britain are "two countries divided by a common language." The aphorism captures a fault line in the discussion of design and content. How can we talk about design and content as if they were separate "places" or things when our experience continually affirms their inseparability? To pull apart the message of a poster (its verbal content and its functional purpose) from its visualization (its embodiment in form, color, and image) completely misses the drama of design, which arises from the way the two parts come together as a unified whole. If we separate design and content for the sake of discussion, we cannot avoid the binarisms that either devalue or over-estimate the importance of form—design as a mode of content in its own right—or of content—the primacy of message, function, and communication.

Within my own practice, the push and pull of design and content has made me shift, at different points, between the prerogatives of an author and the instincts of a dyed-in-the-wool formalist. Many designers experience this split between the hedonism of the eye and the obligations of function, message, and content. Our profession is, in a sense, founded on that gap: we offer ourselves up as people who have the ability to effectively connect form and content. How that connection is made may vary wildly in the hands of different designers, but being a graphic designer depends on one's ability to separate form and content, and then put them back together again. This magic can be performed as a service for others, and you can earn money by doing it well.

As a student at Cooper Union in the early eighties, I was ambivalent about this "service" orientation of design: designers seemed to miss out on the self-determination of artists. Yet I did not believe that my identity was clearly that of an artist either. At Cooper during that period, there was a strong divide between the expressionistic painters and sculptors and the conceptually and politically inclined students who worked across different media. Immersed in critical theory and left politics, I recall being upended by a passage in an essay by Walter Benjamin: "There is no document of culture that is not at the same time a document of barbarism."[1] The phrase haunted me in its suggestion that (as I read it then) the "indulgent" pursuit of art could never be separated from the inequity at the heart of capitalism. This became an uncomfortable soundtrack for my own politicized years at Cooper: with his pronouncement, Benjamin destabilized my attachment to form by imbuing it with an ugly subtext of privilege and hypocrisy.

Yet Benjamin's statement resonated with me because the schizophrenic juxtaposition of poverty and wealth in New York City provided such vivid evidence of the dichotomy he described. During my years in college, I witnessed the extremes of the city, which were especially pronounced at that time (see Tom Wolfe's *The Bonfire of the Vanities*, 1987). During the week I was immersed in classes and lectures at an elite art school and going to art galleries in the boom years of Soho, but on the weekends I rode my bike through the bleakest parts of the city and worked with a program teaching art to disadvantaged New York City high school students.

Although it seems surprising in retrospect, these experiences led me back to the clarity of design and the role of the designer. I liked how the context-driven culture of design immediately placed you at the intersection of form and content. I found myself feeling more confident making "art" that was closer to design in its use of narrative and in its engagement with messages and ideas. I liked design because it seemed to remove the gauzy filter of the artist's identity. My teacher Hans Haacke provided a model of someone whose work was situated in the art world but whose strategies and techniques drew upon design, advertising, and techniques of display. Haacke waged a long battle within the art world: a characteristic early piece traced the provenance of a small painting by Manet of a bundle of asparagus, documenting its complex history of ownership and escalating value, and its intersection with the Nazi regime. *This* was the kind of art I admired, and it was close to the "about-ness" of graphic design.

If the prospect of entering a career in design had a shortcoming, it was that designers seemed less likely to generate the content of their work. "Normal

Mr. Abbott Miller: Twice Removed, 2004

PRINCETON UNIVERSITY SCHOOL OF ARCHITECTURE FALL 1996 LECTURES

MARK COUSINS

THE UGLY

Director of General Studies, Architectural Association London

WED., SEPT. 25, 5:30

MARTHA SCHWARTZ

President, Martha Schwartz Inc.

Adjunct Professor of Landscape Architecture

HARVARD UNIVERSITY GRADUATE SCHOOL OF DESIGN

RECENT WORK

WED., OCT. 2, 5:30

AMY LANDESBERG

Co-principal of Liquid Incorporated and president of Amy Landesberg Architecture

VISITING LECTURER, PRINCETON UNIVERSITY SCHOOL OF ARCHITECTURE

STUNNING ATTRACTIONS: THE HEADROOM, & OTHER NEW WORKS

WED. OCT. 9, 5:30

PETER EISENMAN

FORMING THE INTERSTITIAL

Visiting Professor, Princeton University School of Architecture

WED., OCT. 16, 5:30

ROSALIND KRAUSS

Meyer Shapiro Professor of Modern Art and Theory, History & Archaeology

COLUMBIA UNIVERSITY

FORMLESS: A USER'S GUIDE

WED., NOV. 6, 5:30

ARATA ISOZAKI

THE ISLAND NATION AESTHETIC

Arata Isozaki and Associates, Tokyo, Japan

and

KENZABURO OE

VISITING LECTURER, EAST ASIAN STUDIES DEPARTMENT, PRINCETON UNIVERSITY

WED., NOV. 13, 5:30

ESTHER da Costa MEYER

ASSISTANT PROFESSOR, YALE UNIVERSITY SCHOOL OF ARCHITECTURE

CRUEL METONYMIES: LILLY REICH, PARIS, 1937

WED., NOV. 20, 5:30

WIEL ARETS

Dean of the Berlage Institute, Amsterdam

COUNTER VISUAL

MON., NOV. 25, 5:30

ALL LECTURES TAKE PLACE AT 5:30PM IN BETTS AUDITORIUM ARCHITECTURE BUILDING

ADDITIONAL INFORMATION PLEASE FAX 609-258-4740

e-mail: soa@princeton.edu

internet: http://www.princeton.edu/~soa

LECTURES MADE POSSIBLE BY THE JEAN LABATUT MEMORIAL LECTURE FUND

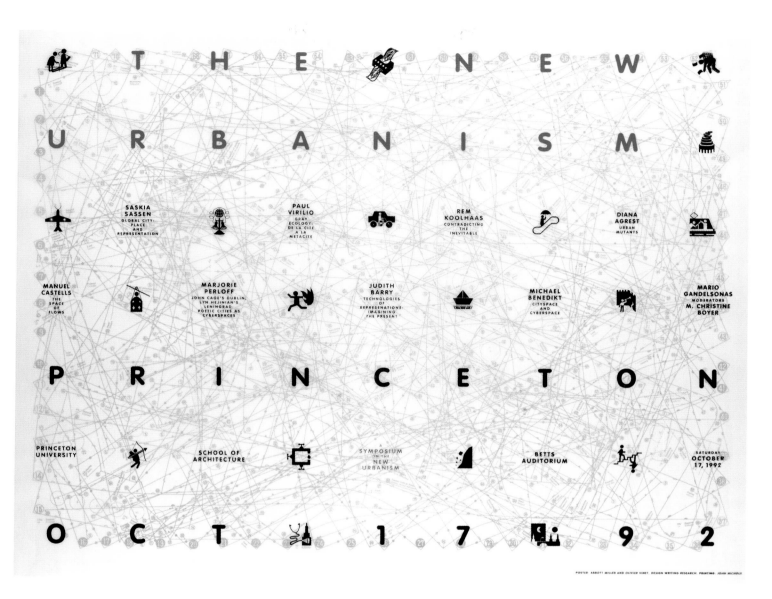

Princeton School of Architecture
Lecture Series poster, 1996

Conference poster for *The New
Urbanism*, 1992

Business card for Design Writing
Research, 1990

NOUVEAU SALON DES CENT EXPOSITION INTERNATIONALE D'AFFICHES. HOMMAGE À TOULOUSE LAUTREC

science" for designers was to use their visual skills to express other peoples' content, whether that content was narrative, commercial, political, or scientific. I wanted to practice design in a way that preserved the self-determination of the artist as the generating force of content. Surely there was a way to be a designer that maintained the engagement and authorship that characterized being an artist.

The historical artists I was most interested in—Marcel Duchamp and Marcel Broodthaers—were conceptualists, unaligned with a specific medium. A number of visiting artists who taught and lectured at Cooper Union—Victor Burgin, Barbara Kruger, Sherrie Levine, Tim Rollins and K.O.S., Joseph Kosuth, Martha Rosler, Michael Asher, Jenny Holzer, Daniel Buren, Barbara Bloom, Louise Lawler, Group Material—incorporated text, photography, and media in their work, providing provocative models of how to negotiate the art/design terrain. If these artists could bend paradigms of art production toward design, I reasoned that I could bend design toward art, or at least to the notion of a practice that follows one's interests and passions as well as meets the needs of clients.

As a student and then as a young designer entering the profession, I was hell-bent on avoiding working for a "typical" design firm, choosing to work with the architect-entrepreneur Richard Saul Wurman, who was relocating his publishing company to New York. This was my way of avoiding the overly defined outcomes of the design studios I knew about. I reasoned that it was better to be in a place focused on publishing its own content. I learned a lot from working with Richard, but I didn't really grow much as a designer because the publications were so heavily templated. Design with a capital *D* was not a priority: instead it was a medium on the way to publishing, and ultimately led to establishing the now well-known TED conferences.

While working for Richard I had opportunities to do freelance projects for a number of art galleries and museums, creating publications, invitations, and advertisements. When I secured a retainer with the New Museum for a year's worth of work, I was able to quit my job and be on my own. I had never worked in a "real" design studio and found myself struggling to define my practice. The available models were vividly staked out in the New York design industry: there

was the cool, conservative Swiss-derived modernism of Rudy de Harak & Associates as well as Chermayeff and Geismar, the Italian rationalism of the Vignellis, the postmodernism of a now less-remembered but influential firm called Doublespace, and the vernacular pastiche and deadpan humor of M&Co, led by Tibor Kalman. I was aware of Pentagram but it registered more dimly as the New York outpost of a British phenomenon.

My stronger reference points were the art galleries that I worked for, the critical theory I read, and my increasing interest in design history. In all of this work I was influenced by Ellen Lupton, who was my friend and classmate and who, after graduating, became curator of a newly established gallery for design, the Herb Lubalin Study Center at Cooper Union. Her base of operation there allowed us to undertake a variety of projects and formulate a practice that we called Design Writing Research.

The DWR studio began as a purely conceptual entity, fueled by intense breakfast meetings in a diner on Astor Place. We progressed to presenting a more legitimate face to clients by borrowing a conference table at Princeton Architectural Press, a small publishing house operating out of a funky townhouse across the street from my even funkier apartment building. From occasionally squatting at their table, we graduated to renting studio space in their back office storage room.

During this time, DWR moved from its basis in small print-based projects to exhibitions and publications. We elaborated our position as a hybrid of think tank, publisher, and design studio. The goal was to fuse our work as designers and writers, creating a studio that could generate content and use the unique skill set of designers to focus on projects about art, design, architecture, and ideas. In this notion of the content-based studio there were a number of inspirational precedents, from Charles and Ray Eames to Quentin Fiore and Bernard Rudofsky.

Our original emphasis on language and theory merged with work for clients who came to us not so much for the manifesto-like pronouncements of our mission, but for the thoughtful interplay of design and content in our projects. DWR was a self-consciously literary and conceptual hothouse version of a design studio, undertaking projects that experimented

Toulouse-Lautrec 100th Anniversary Poster, 2001

with literary theory and psychoanalysis, leaning heavily on what we saw as the vastly underdeveloped relationship between writing and graphic design. We borrowed from Jacques Derrida an expanded notion of "writing" (*écriture*), which included all elements of graphic communication, from symbols to spacing. Hence our predilection for mazes of glyphs, our attentiveness to the minutiae of punctuation, and our maniacal focus on typography and textual systems.

A characteristic project of the moment was a poster Ellen and I designed for a conference at Princeton University's School of Architecture. "The Discourse of the Studio" conference explored the role of language in the development of architectural education. With characteristic glee we burrowed into the language at the heart of it, creating a typographic mise-en-scène. For another Princeton poster on New Urbanism, I created comical International Style symbols overlaid on an old sewing pattern. During those already-bleak years of professional opportunities for architects, I designed a poster representing luminaries of the architecture lecture circuit in the style of classified ads, with a background composed of a pair of Le Corbusier glasses lying on the surface of the help wanted pages of the *New York Times* (in which there were only three jobs posted for architects).

My education at Cooper Union placed me in a very particular position along the design-content axis and gave me a heavily typographic basis. Most of my projects were defined by type and idea, with the occasional use of imagery. After founding my studio I was working on projects that depended purely upon Design with a capital *D*, particularly upon photography and art direction, which were entirely new vocabularies for me. The biggest opportunity in this regard was a magazine called *Dance Ink*, a quarterly publication on dance and performance. The topic was inherently visual, and my role was not as a writer or conceptual agent, but purely as a designer. Presided over by an enlightened publisher, Patricia Tarr; a tolerant editor, Lise Friedman; and a resourceful and well-connected photo editor, Kate Schlesinger, the project became my calling card. Among the magazine's followers were photographers, artists, and performers—an audience that led to related commissions, including a long and formative collaboration with the legendary fashion designer Geoffrey Beene.

Parallel to this emerging design practice was a burgeoning interest in a more academic and research-oriented way of investigating design. In my late twenties I entered a graduate PhD program at the City University of New York. I was able to study with an amazing faculty, deepening my connection to theory and history. During this period there were many opportunities to write, publish, and curate, making this period a fertile combination of practical and theoretical exploration. The academic writing and the work of the studio complemented and reinforced one another. But maintaining a busy studio and graduate studies also collided with adversities in my family: my father became gravely ill and I lost both of my parents in quick succession. It was a difficult period on all fronts.

In time I refocused on maintaining my studio, and Ellen and I worked to reestablish our goals. We took two teaching positions at MICA, the Maryland Institute College of Art. I maintained my studio in New York and set up a parallel studio in Baltimore, beginning a new life as a fluid resident of the eastern corridor. During our first semester in Baltimore, Paula Scher came to MICA as a visiting designer. Paula had joined the New York office of Pentagram in 1991 and, with Michael Bierut and Woody Pirtle, had made it the city's leading design studio, erasing the sense of Pentagram as the stepchild of the London office. I had previously had limited interactions with the Pentagram partners: a couple of years before Paula's visit to MICA, I had written a small piece about her and she had called to tell me that she didn't like it; and although I had previously met Michael Bierut—you can't work in New York without at some point meeting him—I didn't really know him or the other partners at Pentagram.

At MICA, I invited Paula to critique my students' work. As I explained the assignment, she surveyed the posters pinned to the wall. She was a quick study and she charmed the students, even as she ripped them to shreds. And she *had* literally ripped one of the posters to shreds: never one to wait for scissors, she tore a three-by-five-inch fragment from the center of one student's poster and declared, "*There* is a great poster. Try that!"

A month later, Paula invited me to lunch with Michael, and they asked whether I had ever thought of joining Pentagram. In my mind Pentagram was the competition—why would I have thought of joining them when I was busy figuring out how I was different from them? I had never joined anything in my life: no teams, no clubs, no anything. Suddenly a group of talented people were asking me if I wanted to join their practice.

The New York Times Magazine

OCTOBER 3, 2004 / SECTION 6

THE
NEW YORK
ISSUE

HOW
MOMA
WILL
RETELL
THE
STORY OF
MODERNISM
BY ARTHUR LUBOW

**BUILDING
A POST-
INDUSTRY
RECORD
LABEL**
BY RUSSELL SHORTO

TOMORROW'S
BOARD
PLAYERS
PHOTOGRAPHS BY
TINA BARNEY

CAN THERE
EVER BE
A NEXT JOE
PAPP?
BY JESSE GREEN

**MY ART
WORLD**
PAINTINGS AND
DRAWINGS BY
ELIZABETH PEYTON

AND MORE...

THE NEXT CULTURAL
ESTABLISHMENT

Typographic installation for the cover
of the *New York Times Magazine*, 2004.
Photograph by Andrew Moore

15

Sunny sides, 2012. Handmade by glass
artisans at Corning Museum GlassLab

It took me a year to figure it out, but I found myself drawn to the idea of having partners, of having three-dimensional disciplines within the culture of the studio and learning how a "real" studio worked. I was convinced that I could bring something specific to Pentagram and that I could benefit—intellectually, financially, and emotionally—from Pentagram's unique work paradigm. Certain projects I've taken on since joining Pentagram are classic DWR projects combining curating, writing, and designing, while others bear the influence—whether through their environmental scale or their populist character—of a Pentagram ethos.

Across the changes of geography, studio spaces, and clients, my goal has always been to capture a reciprocity between design and content. Design is not a passive presentation of already cooked and digested ideas, but a critical tool, capable of creating its own insights. This notion of design rests on an active and less hierarchical conception of practice—a model closer to a collective search between author, curator, and designer.

Design is a conceptual tool, a kind of metalanguage operating alongside and somewhat "above" writing, and a bit outside of rational thinking. Design thinking offers an alternative to sequential, expository, and reasoned thought processes. The prerogatives of design—visual correspondence; visual impact; contrast of scale, materiality, form, and color—bring you into communication problems from a different perspective. Design thinking dissolves the lines between form and content, and between two and three dimensions. The duality of design—its status as a discourse in its own right, as well as being a medium for discovery—positions designers as interpreters and performers of content.

Design animates and enables: a powerful design concept is something that is "owned" and "used" by everyone working on a project. I love the moment—if it happens—when everyone involved in a project gets behind a design because it has the force of inevitability. Once you've alighted on a premise, it starts to make its own arguments and shows you how to move forward. A powerful design concept has an almost palpable current that pushes a project along.

Because so many design decisions are formal and arbitrary—which doesn't make them trivial—it is deeply satisfying when you hit upon a visual, spatial, or narrative rationale for a design endeavor. Establishing this governing concept helps ground the work, rooting it in a logic that unfolds on its own. This phase of any project is the period of greatest invention. I've learned that you'd better have your fun in those exploratory moments, because those flashes of insight require months and years of meetings, flights, emails, and approvals to see the light of day.

Negotiating the relationship between design and content is the defining dynamic of my work. The material presented in this book covers a broad spectrum of practice in the cultural arena—identity, exhibition, environmental, and publication design. Seen in proximity, the individual projects communicate with each other across time and disciplines. With its emphasis on meaning and context, my work makes content legible through form. Style is not the place where design begins, but something that happens along the way, as an echo of content. To find it, the designer must listen and look, read and write, teasing out the messages that reverberate against the surfaces of what we know.

1. Walter Benjamin, "Theses on the Philosophy of History," in *Illuminations*, ed. Hannah Arendt, New York, Schocken Books, 1969.

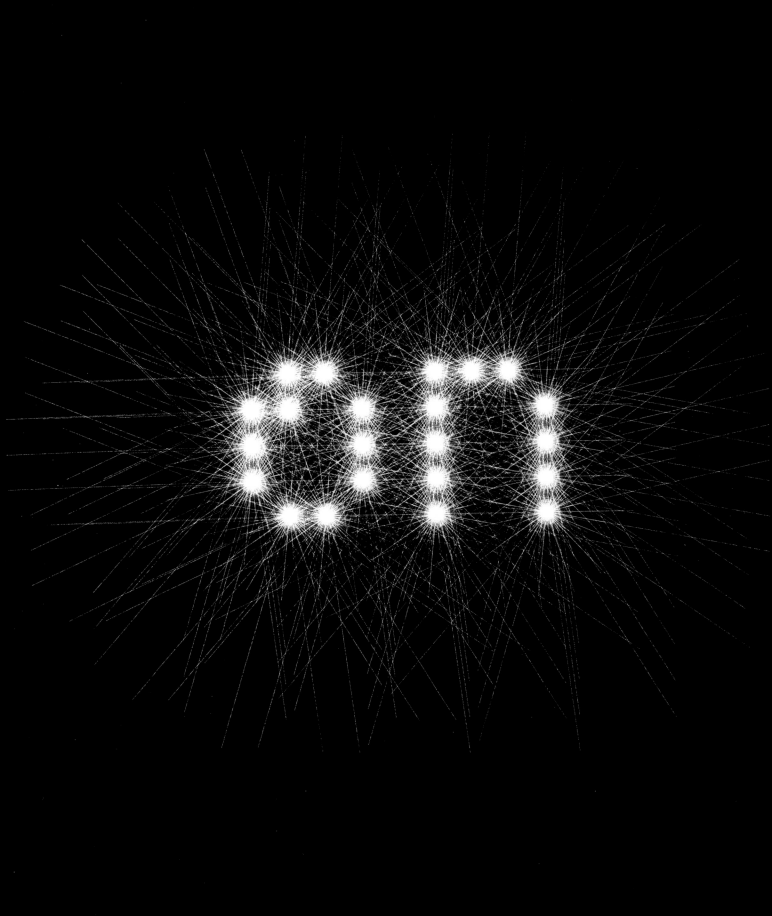

the archaeology of college

ELLEN LUPTON

Slim, blond, and dressed with a gently disheveled formality, Abbott Miller was used to getting hassled on the streets of New York City. One time, he got mugged. It was the summer of 1980, and he had come all the way from Indiana to study in the high school summer program at Parsons School of Design. Abbott wasn't a hayseed—his hometown was just outside Chicago, a city he often visited in search of museums and foreign films. But in the context of Union Square, he exuded an excruciating innocence that begged to be roughed up.

Back then the area around 14th Street was a hub for dealers and prostitutes: there was no Greenmarket, no Starbucks, no Dean & deLuca, no multiplexes or triple-decker strollers. Abbott was walking up a crowded side street one sticky day in July when two teenagers pulled a knife on him and demanded his money. Abbott took his wallet out of his back pocket and handed it over to the kid with the knife, who flipped it open and yelled into Abbott's face, "Shit, this thing is empty," and threw it back at him. As his assailants fled, he reached into his front pocket. Safely folded there was his meager wad of cash.

Getting mugged wasn't the kindest introduction to life in New York, but Abbott returned the following year to attend college at the Cooper Union—just a few blocks east of Parsons. Abbott lived in a Chelsea brownstone owned by a Quaker woman who was the widow of a famous mathematician. She ran her house like a salon, hosting monthly dinners for writers, composers, and artists. Abbott survived on vegetables that he cooked in an electric wok. He got so skinny he wore two pairs of underwear—boxers *and* briefs—to keep his pants from falling down. He rarely drank, never smoked, and wasn't interested in girls. (A few girls tried, and some guys too, but no one could get close to this pale blond boy from Indiana.) His devotion to his work bordered on the extreme. During freshman year, when other students were struggling to forget what they'd learned in high school, Abbott was building sculptures with found objects, imbuing everything he touched with a luxurious yet alienated domesticity. I was a freshman too, in the same sculpture class, barely grasping the skills to make any 3-D object worth talking about.

In our first-year sculpture class, Abbott constructed a sculpture out of two wooden doors he found on the street. He cut the first door into little rectangles that were the same proportion as the other door. He spread the little doors on the floor in a low pile and laid the big door on top. The concept, he explained, reflected his childhood belief that every object is made up of molecules shaped like that object. Chairs are made of chair-molecules, hats are made of hat-molecules, and so on.

Abbott had meticulously stripped, sanded, and painted the doors—the big one and all the little ones—to make them match each other as closely as possible. This procedure consumed dozens of hours—all for a one-week assignment. Niki Logis, our loud spoken, bullshit-resistant teacher, took pleasure in Abbott's whole-hearted endeavors while laughing at them just a little. "Stripping and painting those doors," she said, "that's decorating." An artist wouldn't bother with that. An artist would just cut up the goddamn door.

Niki's course became Abbott's most important laboratory. For one project, he salvaged a wooden shutter and some slender newel posts. He used the newel posts to support the shutter at a gentle incline, turning its slats into a tiny flight of stairs. Another week, he found a rusty box spring and a pile of twisted metal studs. He stuck the studs into the coils of the box spring, making them jut out at wild angles. He spray-painted the whole ensemble silver before installing it in the gleaming men's room near the dean's office. He hung the piece right next to the urinals, its jagged edges thrusting toward the urinals. The class critique convened in the men's room.

One of Niki's assignments was to construct long, rectangular box beams out of thin sheets of composite board and combine them with sturdy cardboard tubes, easily found on the street. Abbott's piece was over six feet tall and employed dozens of elements. In the woodshop, Niki showed us how to cut the sides of our box beams on the table saw and then glue and nail them together. This was a reasonable task under ordinary circumstances, but Abbott proceeded with his characteristic compulsion, setting a brad every two inches along each seam of the box. Tripling the normal number of nails would demand hours of menial attention, but there was no turning back. The unity of the piece required an even rhythm of nails; he couldn't possibly skimp on brads just to save time.

On/Off, 1999. Photogravure print

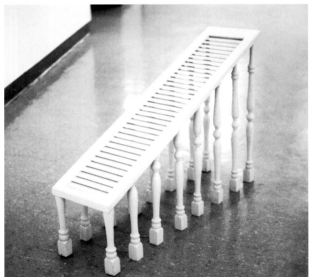

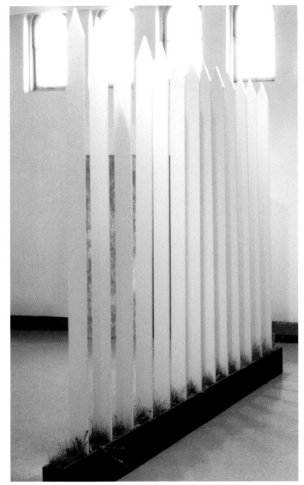

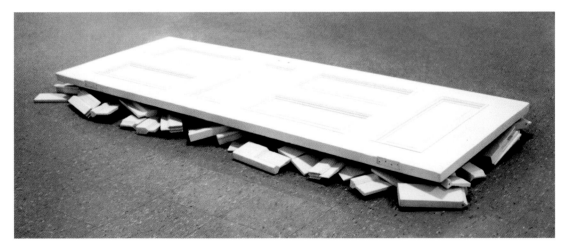

Stair, 1981. Shutter and newel posts

Picket, 1981. Wooden pickets painted with white enamel, in a trough filled with dirt and grass

Door, 1981. Wooden door resting on sawn door fragments

problem is design solving

fred gates
ellen lupton
jerry abbott miller
eileen o'neill

senior show
at the cooper union's houghton gallery
seven east seventh street second floor

the show will open on may thirteenth at six pm

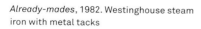

Already-mades, 1982. Westinghouse steam iron with metal tacks

Stud Mattress, 1981. Coil mattress and metal studs, installed in a men's restroom

Exhibition invitation, 1985. Offset printing on white #10 window envelope

Abbott Miller, 1982. Photograph by Eileen O'Neill

Chairs, 1982. Canvas stretched over chairbacks, painted with gesso

(The brads were free, anyway, dispensed from a big bucket near the hand tools.)

Abbott still had twelve or so beams to nail together when I offered to help. It was seven o'clock on a Thursday night. I had made short shrift of my own half-assed sculpture, so I had plenty of time to spare. "That's a lot of nails you've got there, buddy," I said. "Can I help?" He said sure, and for the next few hours we hunched together over his box beams with two hammers and a cup of nails. Working there in the dusty rumble of the woodshop, I felt at once intrigued and repelled by this brainy, ethereal man-child with his milky blue shirt buttoned up to the chin. Like those kids on 14th Street, I wanted—in some dim part of me—to smack him, to shake his spun-sugar shoulders and dislodge his exasperating perfectionism. Feeling at once elated and doomed, I knew without doubt—that night building box beams—that I loved him.

It would take Abbott seven years to love me back. In the meantime, we would work side by side as friends, no benefits, pursuing a journey that still defines us as designers and writers. Many Cooper students viewed graphic design as a safe and predictable career path. Design was a trade to be learned, lacking the grandeur and risks of the art world. Many of the school's design majors came from the New York area; many had parents in the industry. They were insiders who knew what they wanted.

Outsiders like Abbott—who weren't certain about becoming designers at all—had a different perspective. Desktop computers hadn't yet started changing the nature of the craft, and the design scene lacked the intellectual energy it has today. Graphic design classes attracted kids who were neat, who could draw that proverbial straight line and lay down perfect arcs with a French curve. Abbott was neat, exceedingly so, but he also had a sharp critical mind that was steeped in conceptual art and experimental film.

This was a period of discord in the New York art world. The booming market for neo-expressionist painting garnered disgust from a new generation of socially oriented artists who had come out of the conceptual art movement. Barbara Kruger, Sherrie Levine, Richard Prince, and Jenny Holzer were using photography and text to question the structures of art, power, and consumption. "Protect me from what I want," announced one of Holzer's photocopied truisms, pasted onto signs and telephone poles around the East Village. "The future is stupid."

Hans Haacke, a German émigré who taught at Cooper, was a widely respected conceptual artist with a politically engaged practice. Haacke's advanced sculpture courses imparted no technical skills and assigned no projects. Students brought in work and the group would talk about it. Abbott signed up for Hans's course in sophomore year, entering a den of die-hard Haacke acolytes (called "Haackettes" by their detractors). Everyone in the group leaned reflexively left, disdaining any work that smacked of middle-class complacency or commodification. Physical objects were under general suspicion. Market appeal was verboten. Practicing art at all was increasingly problematic. The Haackettes were juniors and seniors who spoke with self-satisfied intellectual superiority and Abbott was fresh blood.

This scene was way more intimidating than Niki's Sculpture 101. The first project Abbott presented in Haacke's class was his chair paintings. He had collected a dozen or so abandoned chairs and hauled them up to the woodshop, where he carefully sawed off their backs, wrapped the backrests in canvas, and primed them with white gesso. Abbott lavished acute care upon this humble task, pulling the canvas perfectly taut around each wooden carcass before painting and sanding the surfaces to create smooth and faceless monoliths. Soft shadows appeared where the canvas strained against a raised ridge or slowly cresting curve.

Abbott installed his chair paintings in a row and waited for class to begin. When the group finally assembled, the Haackettes dismissed the chair paintings as empty works of bourgeois décor. To begin with, anything that called itself a painting deserved enhanced interrogation, since the entire medium of painting had slipped into mordant irrelevance. Abbott's paintings were especially infuriating because they arrived cloaked in an aura of conceptual art yet offered no political or social commentary.

Scolded by his schoolmates, Abbott coined the term "apartment art." After all, he had an apartment and he needed art. Wasn't there a place for that? Looking at his chair paintings—curtly dismissed as ornamental upholstery—he saw that indeed, much of his work was about functional objects and spaces. Architects and designers seemed at peace with enhancing daily life; what made artists so afraid?

Abbott tried showing the chair pieces in an advanced painting class to see how they fared in another context. The painters were a different crowd—more relaxed, less political, speaking their own smooth lingo. The painters greeted Abbott's chair paintings with a warm and tolerant enthusiasm that was completely off mark. They urged him to add paint and pigment to the pieces, exploring the picture plane with light and shadow. Work the surface, they said. Amplify the illusion. Pump up the tension between canvas and support. Yet Abbott's projects were not about a painter's dynamic of push and pull. There was no illusion. There was only the object and the obsessive exactitude of its making.

Embarking on more narrative work, Abbott created an installation about Union Square Park. He juxtaposed news accounts of drug busts, riots, and demonstrations with images of turn-of-the-century engravings depicting the park as an urban pastoral with trees, squirrels, and cast-iron benches. The piece also relayed Abbott's own story about getting mugged near the park. When he showed it in class the older Haackettes saw the piece as enforcing stereotypes. The work, they said, could be misinterpreted as classist, racist, and nostalgic. The broader story of urban transformation was lost among the details. As Abbott took down his newspaper clippings and photocopies, the work itself looked wan and gray. Regardless of the project's perceived politics, these slips of paper were devoid of material intrigue. They told a story but lacked form and presence.

By the end of sophomore year Abbott turned to graphic design, enrolling in courses with the intimidating Czech modernist George Sadek while continuing to experiment with art. Now he would bring art and theory to bear on design, rather than the other way around. The career track for a gallery artist didn't seem any less commercial than becoming a designer. Abbott sat in on Barbara Kruger's classes at Cooper Union. She said, "People, please, do not be naive about the marketplace." She had once worked as a designer at *Mademoiselle* but was now gaining attention for her photo-based work and beginning to show at Mary Boone Gallery. For Abbott this was a come-to-Jesus moment—the art world was as commercialized as design.

Abbott showed his chair paintings one more time at Cooper Union, in a student exhibition organized with other design outsiders (Fred Gates, Eileen O'Neill, and myself). The college had recently hosted a traveling exhibition called Design Is Problem Solving; the show's somber message was that design is always about solving an issue or addressing a human need. That's what makes design different from art. Abbott defiantly titled our own impromptu show *Problem Is Design Solving*. He printed empty business envelopes with the exhibition title in eight point Helvetica as a return address. His grandmother later complained that he had sent her a letter with nothing in it.

The chair paintings didn't solve a problem; they questioned the space between painting and sculpture, furniture and art, sameness and difference. If Abbott was going to be a designer, he wasn't going to do it by solving somebody's problems. He saw design as part of cultural production in general, where he was less like a translator and more like an interpreter.

Abbott would continue to needle the earnest platitudes of the profession. In the mid-1990s, he would return to Cooper to organize exhibitions and events such as the Aspirin Design Conference, a daylong performance in Cooper's Great Hall. The conference poked fun at the historic Aspen Design Conference, an annual gathering of elite designers: Chip Kidd was the emcee wandering the aisles in his woolen knickers with a mobile microphone like an Edwardian Dr. Phil; Art Club 2000 assembled IKEA furniture on stage; and Mike Mills charted the checkered history of Herbert Bayer's universal typeface. Bayer had emigrated to the United States in the 1930s and helped found the Aspen Design Conference. The conference program featured the universal typeface and a mountain of Bayer Aspirin with cotton clouds that re-created the iconic black and yellow cover of CliffsNotes.

Fueling the levity was an interest in critical theory. At Cooper, we were reading philosophy and film theory in courses taught by the critic P. Adams Sitney: Kant and Hegel, Heidegger and Freud, Stan Brakhage and Hollis Frampton. My twin sister Julia—a humanities major at Johns Hopkins University and then a PhD student at Yale—fed us cutting-edge texts on semiotics and deconstruction. As we saw it, French theory kept circling back to issues of design. The archaeology of knowledge, the death of the author, the materiality of writing, the empire of signs, the thick opacity of white space, the monotonous duplicity of the simulacrum—each of these concepts had design squatting in its margins.

For his graduation show, Abbott juxtaposed his longstanding interests in cinema studies and cultural

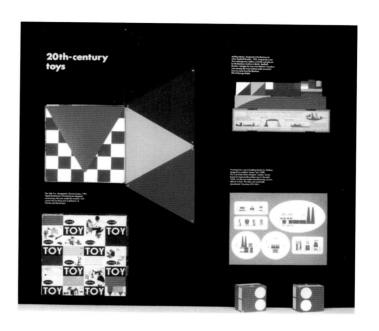

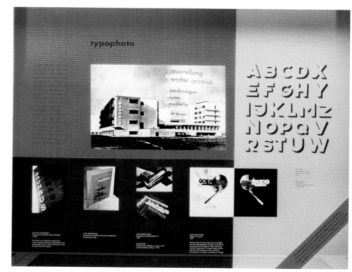

Aspirin Design Conference
program, 1994

Details from the exhibition
*The ABC's of ▲■●: The Bauhaus
and Design Theory*, 1991

Design Writing Research: Writing on Graphic Design, originally published in 1996, has been translated into multiple languages.

history. From film theory he borrowed the notion of the cinematic "apparatus" as a medium whose power is derived, in part, from holding the viewer captive in a darkened room. In Foucault's *Discipline and Punish*, he saw parallels to cinema in the Panopticon, a prison design from the Enlightenment in which cells radiate around a central observation tower. For Foucault, the Panopticon initiated a uniquely modern, internalized dynamic of hidden control and surveillance. A determined researcher, Abbott journeyed to Stateville Correctional Center in Joliet, Illinois, a maximum-security prison built on the Panopticon model. (There, the guards in the central watchtower were equipped with rifles and were completely visible to the inmates.) Abbott linked the invention of film with the power relations of the Panopticon, producing his installation on a series of window shades.

Foucault's *Archaeology of Knowledge* continued to drive our work after Cooper. We enrolled in the art history PhD program at the City University of New York, where we studied with Rosalind Krauss and Rosemarie Haag Bletter. Although we both left graduate school after a few years, we were able to turn our research and writing into a stream of published essays, books, and exhibitions in the early 1990s. Kevin Lippert, a young graduate of Princeton's School of Architecture, was running an independent press out of a building across the street from our apartment on East 7th Street. Kevin published our first books, *The ABC's of ▲■●: The Bauhaus and Design Theory* (an archaeology of design education) and *The Bathroom, the Kitchen, and the Aesthetics of Waste: A Process of Elimination* (a psychobiography of industrial design). We've been collaborating with Kevin and Princeton Architectural Press ever since.

Published in 1992, *A Process of Elimination* accompanied an exhibition we curated at MIT's List Visual Arts Center. Through the lens of Freudian theory our show examined the emergence of the modern kitchen and bathroom. The project examined the consumerist compulsion to buy and replace goods as it coincided with new and improved technologies for managing food and waste in the home—from gas stoves and built-in kitchens to plumbed bathtubs and flush toilets.

A Process of Elimination reflected our own psychobiographies as well. Our protracted Victorian-style courtship had finally been consummated after seven years of strangled lust, suppressed desire, and

midnight sessions setting type on an archaic Compugraphics system. In 1988, those years of incessant longing on my part (and of celestial indifference on his) erupted at last in sexual congress, rapid cohabitation, and, in 1990, marriage. Our research for *A Process of Elimination* divided along strict gender lines: I did the kitchen and he did the bathroom.

Following the kitchen and bathroom show, Abbott organized an exhibition called Printed Letters: A Natural History of Typography, in which he designed a massive display table divided into compartments like a job case for holding metal type. Abbott filled the cases with printing specimens, lead type, and taxidermied animals. Typography, the exhibition proclaimed, is a museum of the word: a graphical inventory of fossilized traces. Language had been slaughtered, stuffed, and put on display by the system of alphabetic writing. To Abbott's delight, the show enraged a writer for the *New York Times*, who denounced it for being "elegant to the point of stylishness" and for "arousing anxiety in those who, like the reviewer, are behind in their Structuralism."

As students, Abbott and I characterized our practice as "design-writing-research." Design, we concluded, is a form of writing: it encompasses text (since all writing is visual) while also engaging space, margin, grid, image, and architecture. Abbott named his first studio Design Writing Research, established a few years after we graduated from Cooper. The same phrase became the title of our book *Design Writing Research: Writing on Graphic Design*, a designer-as-author manifesto. These collected essays applied critical theory to graphic design, dissecting such subversive events as the legendary collaboration between designer Quentin Fiore and Marshall McLuhan, who coauthored the radical *The Medium is the Massage*.

Abbott has turned his preoccupations into a practice that bears the imprint of his past. A fascination with psychic dwelling governs his work and life. The melancholic domesticity of those early sculptures and exhibitions inhabits our home, originally built as a social club in 1916. In the "gathering room," where club members once assembled for drinks and conversation, Abbott's chair paintings hang above a series of French doors. They gaze down on us like ghostly dinner guests, their canvas skins shrouding their identities while exposing the human variation that can be found, if you are looking, in a crowd of anonymous things.

LACTOSE INTOLERANT

CHALKY RESIDUE

MORNING SICKNESS

AMBIGUOUS DIFFERENCE

DANDRUFF

POWDERED WHIG

INHIBITION

AGGRESSIVE BEIGE

ASPIRIN

STOLEN IVORY

CLOTTED ARTERY

WHITE PRIVILEGE

"White Space," *Print* magazine, 2007. Photograph by Jay Zukerkorn

design is a mode of inquiry

I think every designer entertains fantasies of life without editors or clients standing between you and the project as you see it. The work shown on the following pages represents some of my most rewarding projects because I was able to function as a designer, writer, and curator, using design as a mode of inquiry into a particular subject. My first studio Design Writing Research named an intention to weave these three activities together, seeking a model of design practice that enabled the studio to function like a laboratory that would advance writing and research on design-related topics, extending the boundaries of traditional design practice. By its very nature the model implied a loop of activity where research feeds into writing, which leads to its realization in the form of exhibitions and publications. Museums and galleries have provided a forum for this practice, offering opportunities to explore connections between curating, designing, and publishing.

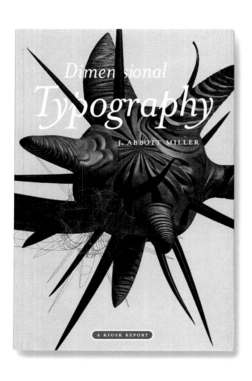

Dimensional Typography, 1996

Detail of a dimensional lowercase *j* we developed based on the typeface JesusLovesYouAll by Lucas de Groot. The detail shows the letterform seen from overhead.

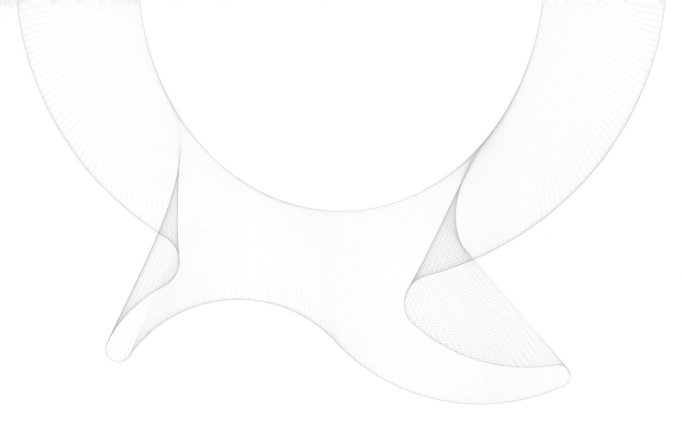

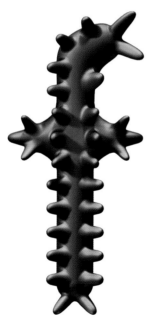

Detail of the letter *Q* where the tail is generated by a ripple in the fabric of the letter.

A dimensional lowercase *f* was based on the knobby silhouette of Zuzana Licko's 1995 font Modula Ribbed.

A rendering of a Bodoni *A* reinterprets its thick-and-thin characteristics as an effect of intersecting planes.

dimensional typography

In 1996, Claudia Gould, then director of Artists Space, invited me to create an exhibition. I developed a specific body of work about the impact of digital technology on type. The exhibition, called Exhibit A: Design, Writing, Research, displayed visualizations of type conceived in three dimensions. The project explored the sculptural properties of letters, inspired by the experiential qualities of virtual environments.

Our case studies included historic and experimental letterforms, building on the implied physicality of classic fonts like Bodoni, as well as contemporary typefaces such as JesusLovesYouAll by Lucas de Groot and Modula Ribbed by Zuzana Licko. We developed ideas in the studio through drawings and paper models that provided the basis for digital renderings that we commissioned from a range of people working in the relatively new arena of 3-D software. We exhibited the wireframes and renderings as transparencies on medical x-ray light boxes, presenting the work in the context of a luminous screen and implying a microscopic universe of typographic organisms capable of growing and propagating like cells or root systems. I created a small book, *Dimensional Typography: Words in Space*, that documented the project and has served as a point of departure for a number of related investigations and exhibitions.

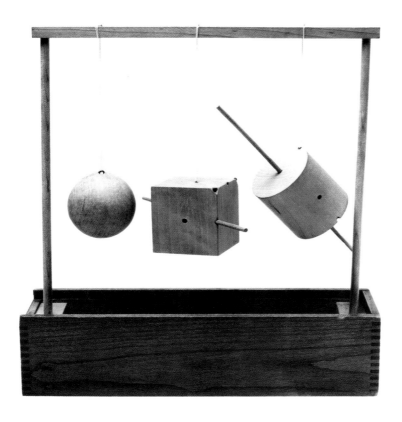

the abc's of ▲■●

Developed with Ellen Lupton, *The ABC's of* ▲■●: *The Bauhaus and Design Theory* (1991) explored the origins and impact of the Bauhaus. The exhibition and publication, produced at the Cooper Union, analyzed the Bauhaus's preoccupation with the circle, square, and triangle, and primary colors as a foundational grammar of modern design. The project examined the prehistory of the Bauhaus through educational reforms in art education, particularly the radical pedagogy of Friedrich Froebel's kindergarten, which used elementary shapes and colors as building blocks in a progressive education process. The notion that one could breakdown the visual world into its basic parts and elaborate a "language of vision" was integral to Bauhaus theory. The project considered this concept critically and looked at its influence on succeeding generations of designers, educators, and schools in the United States.

In the original edition of the book Herbert Bayer's geometrically derived font universal was featured on the cover and produced in letterpress. The pages of the book were stitched in alternating yellow, red, and blue thread.

A **graph** plots data in a gridded space, whose axes represent variables such as time, temperature, or quantity. Many **graphs** depict change over time with a linear mark, as in a sine curve or a "fever" chart. The **graph** belongs to the category of signs called the **index**, which has a causal relationship to its referent. For example, a photograph, a footprint, or a shadow is an index, because it results from physical contact with an object. An arrow is an index, because its meaning in any given instance depends on its proximity to an object. Indexical signs appear throughout the textbooks of Klee, Kandinsky, and Moholy-Nagy; they serve as potential characters in a universal script that would have a direct link to the physical or spiritual world.

In the basic design textbooks of Klee and Kandinsky, the **graph** is a model of pictorial expression. Whereas the geometry of Euclid defines a **line** as an infinite accumulation of static **points**, the design primers of Klee and Kandinsky describe the line as a single point dragged across a page: the line is a trace of the artist's motion, a spatial index or **graph** of a temporal event. Similarly, a **plane** is the record left by a moving line. The diagram below, from Klee's *Pedagogical Sketchbook*, maps this temporal narrative; Klee employs a a linguistic metaphor, comparing phases in the life of a point to the *"active and passive voice"* in speech. The language of vision is written with indexical signs.

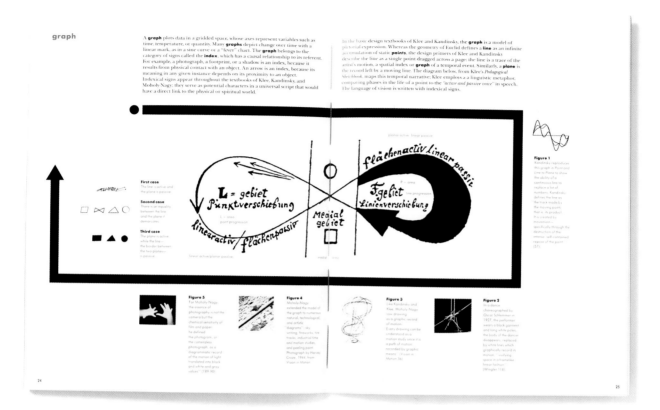

First case
The line is active and the plane is passive.

Second case
There is an equality between the line and the plane: it demonstrates.

Third case
The plane is active while the line – the border between the two planes – is passive.

Figure 1
Kandinsky reproduces this graph in *Point and Line to Plane* to show the ability of a continuous line to replace a lot of numbers. Kandinsky defines the line as the track made by the moving point, that is, its product. It is created by movement – specifically through the destruction of the intense, self-contained repose of the point (57).

Figure 5
For Moholy-Nagy, the essence of photography is not the camera but the chemical sensitivity of film and paper. he defined the photogram, or the cameraless photograph, as a diagrammatic record of the motion of light translated into black and white and grey values" (189-90)

Figure 4
Moholy-Nagy extended the model of the graph to numerous natural, technological, and artistic "diagrams": dry writing, fireworks, tire tracks, industrial lines and motion studies. Photograph by Harvey Croze, 1944, from *Vision in Motion*

Figure 3
Like Kandinsky and Klee, Moholy-Nagy saw drawing as a graphic record of motion. Every drawing can be understood as a motion study since it is a path of motion recorded by graphic means (*Vision in Motion* 36)

Figure 2
In a dance choreographed by Oscar Schlemmer in 1927, the performer wears a black garment and long white poles; the body of the dancer disappears, replaced by white lines which graphically record its motion, "evolving space in a framelike linear fashion" (Wingler 118)

the abc's of ▲■●

the bauhaus and design theory

The Herb Lubalin Study Center of Design and Typography The Cooper Union for the Advancement of Science and Art

An educational toy designed by Friedrich Froebel, included in the exhibition

A display vitrine with objects from the kindergarten movement

A spread and cover from *The ABC's of ▲■●: The Bauhaus and Design Theory,* 1991

printed letters

Jersey City, New Jersey, was once the center of the typesetting industry thanks to American Type Founders, a company that was the Standard Oil of metal type production. The sprawling factory supplied metal type for the pressrooms of the world but succumbed to the photographic—then digital—revolutions that transformed type into increasingly immaterial "information." Printed Letters: The Natural History of Typography (1992), exhibited at the Jersey City Museum, presented the aesthetic and technological issues surrounding type production, explaining the rapid rise and fall of this local industry.

Inspired by the work of Michel Foucault—particularly his analysis of classification systems—I used the metaphor of natural history to explain how typography preserves words on a page, similar to the way specimens are preserved in a natural history museum.

The exhibition reveled in the heterogeneous mixture of natural history displays and "cabinets of curiosity." The "cabinet" was based on the gridded trays ("job case") used to sort metal type. The exhibition juxtaposed natural and typographic "specimens," making analogies between lead type and mineral artifacts. The inscription that forms a frieze around the room stated that "typography is a museum of the word" and that "the word is a form of fossilized speech." A historic rendering of the ATF factory looms in the background, an image of the distant past of Jersey City. The antiquarian aesthetic, complete with potted palms (à la Marcel Broodthaers), was intended to conjure a funereal aura, appropriate to the loss of industry, as well as a paean to the passing of type as a corporeal thing.

Installation view of Printed Letters: The Natural History of Typography, 1992

CH TO ENDURE OVER TIME LIKE THE SHELLS, BONES & DEAD INSECTS COLLECTED IN A NATURAL HISTORY MUSEUM. PRINTED

Cover of *The Bathroom, the Kitchen, and the Aesthetics of Waste: A Process of Elimination*, 1992

the process of elimination

In the 1920s and 1930s, domestic theorists, economists, and designers conceptualized the American household as an organism that could be understood through analogies to the human body. Our exhibition and book *The Bathroom, the Kitchen, and the Aesthetics of Waste: A Process of Elimination* (1992) looked at consumption and waste as literal, bodily processes that form a template for our consumption of products, and thus reflect these cycles in the larger economy. Commissioned by the List Visual Arts Center at MIT, the project argued that many of the innovations, materials, and aesthetics of modern design originated in the bathroom and kitchen—that modernism entered the home through the back door, led through the technological innovations of water supply and waste removal.

A series of case studies on the toilet, sink, stove, and refrigerator presented the shift from "furniture-based" typologies to "fixture-based" forms from the turn of the century to the 1940s. The parallel emergence of the modern kitchen and bathroom—sharing plumbing as well as nonporous surfaces and built-in elements—was viewed against the cultural habit of seeing these two engines of the home as separate.

The "process of elimination" referred to both the stylistic reduction of modern design and the corporeal reality of waste as a corollary to consumption. The exhibition design used the vernacular of open stud walls to underscore their shared technologies. To heighten the thematic of cleanliness and waste, we displayed the objects on beds of moist dirt. A centerpiece of the show was an elaborate turn-of-the-century bathroom, installed on a floor tiled with 1,500 bars of Ivory soap.

In the early 20th century, the bathroom and kitchen shifted from the margins to the center of the home. These newly equipped spaces for managing waste set a hygienic standard for the rest of the household.

The imperative for clean bodies and houses has fueled an endless appetite for new products. Just as sexual pleasure is propped on the organs of digestion, the restless desire for new goods is built upon the obsessive routines surrounding biological consumption.

...eud describes how ...e organs of digestion. ...monly viewed as ...antile pleasure, articulated ...the mouth and anus ..., washing, and wiping.

STREAMLINING
The Aesthetics of Waste

A bathroom diorama featuring turn-of-the-century fixtures from *The Bathroom, the Kitchen, and the Aesthetics of Waste: A Process of Elimination*, MIT List Visual Arts Center, Cambridge, MA, 1992

A spread from *The Bathroom, the Kitchen, and the Aesthetics of Waste: A Process of Elimination*

brick book

Echoing the eighteenth-century tradition of *architecture parlante*, in which a building visually expresses its function, I was interested in making a book that represented a brick but also functioned like a brick. Based on the size and shape of standard American bricks, each *Brick Book* (1997) is drilled with the characteristic three-hole pattern. The edges have been hand-painted so that when stacked into a series of constructions—as they were exhibited at the Andrea Rosen Gallery—they create the visual texture of a masonry wall. The object makes an implicit comparison between bricks as a unit of construction and books as a unit of knowledge; both create physical and symbolic structures. Various processes of bookmaking (binding, trimming, drilling, embossing) were employed in their production, but they intentionally avoid offset printing.

Installation and detail of *Brick Book*, Andrea Rosen Gallery, New York, 1997

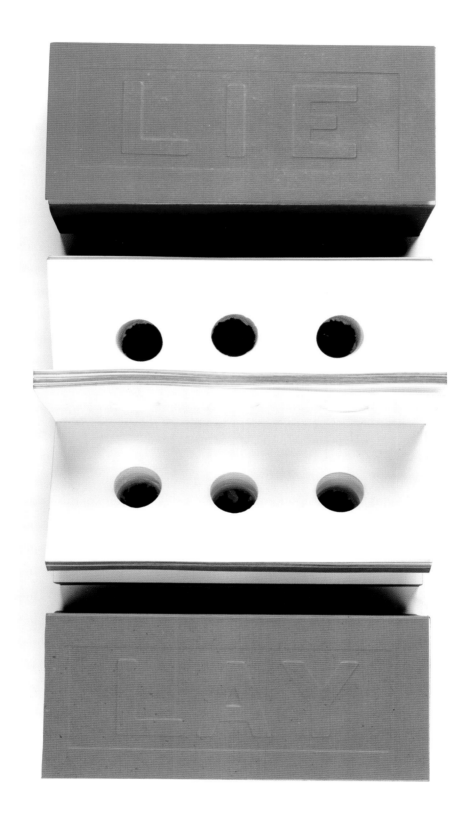

up, down, across

Upon entering the exhibition Up, Down, Across: Elevators, Escalators, and Moving Sidewalks (2003), visitors were confronted by a large elevator with motion sensors that activated sliding doors. Once inside, elevator music (Muzak) accompanied a short film that analyzed elevator behavior. A second set of doors opened onto a bright yellow gallery dominated by life-size symbols of "people movers." These icons anchored the exhibition's thematic zones of the elevator, escalator, and moving sidewalk. The emphatic visual character of

the exhibition, held at the National Building Museum, was a response to the heterogeneous content; architectural models, fragments, photographs, film clips, and many other artifacts required an environment that united these items as facets of one overarching theme of conveyance.

The second half of the exhibition presented a survey of architectural projects that foreground circulation as an integral part of a building's form and identity. Drawings, photographs, and models showed how architects have incorporated people movers, tracing a

shift toward "expressive conveyance" initiated in the 1970s with the famous Centre Georges Pompidou in Paris. The exhibition followed this trajectory into the present with projects that embrace the technology of conveyance as central, even formative, to the design of a building. Architect Rem Koolhaas's statement that "architecture can finally be unmasked for what it is: flow" is indicative of how the issue of conveyance has moved from the margins to the center of the built environment.

Installation views of *Up, Down, Across*, National Building Museum, Washington, D.C., 2003

brno echo

Brno Echo: Ornament and Crime from Adolf Loos to Now (2008) was an installation I curated and designed at the Moravian Gallery, a museum in Brno, Czech Republic. The exhibition coincided with the 23rd International Biennial of Graphic Design Brno. The project staged a dialogue between historical and contemporary design on the topic of "modern ornament."

Beginning with the original 1963 biennial logo by designer Jiří Hadlač, I traced the history of concentric stripes in modern design. Adolf Loos, who was born in Brno, wrote *Ornament and Crime*, a 1908 manifesto that served as the conceptual foundation for the exhibition. Looking at stripes as a recurrent grammar of modern ornament, the exhibition connected everything from the Wiener Werkstätte to Pop Art to retro-futurism.

The exhibition and book created a graphic echo chamber in which typefaces, posters, textiles, and furniture revealed a cosmopolitan dialogue that crossed time and place. Drawing upon international sources and the collections of the Moravian Gallery, the installation featured a dozen galleries and over 150 works, including a large model of Loos's famous unbuilt Josephine Baker House from 1928. Each gallery featured a large wall of historic or contemporary wallpaper. The poster I designed for the exhibition took Hadlač's *B* and extended it into the title of the show. Wall texts featured statements from artists, designers, and writers commenting on the nature of repetition in contemporary life and the constant recirculation of forms and images.

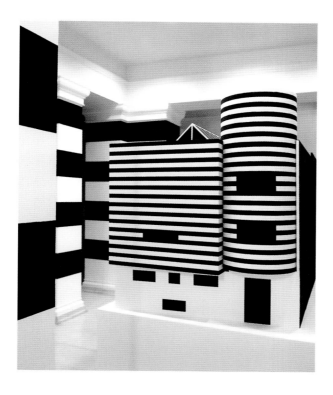

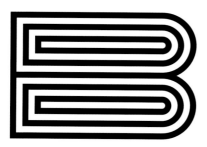

Installation view of poster wall and Thonet chairs from Brno Echo, Moravian Gallery, Brno, Czech Republic, 2008

A view of the gallery with a large model of the Josephine Baker House, designed by Adolf Loos

The logo for the 1963 Brno Biennial, designed by Jiří Hadlač

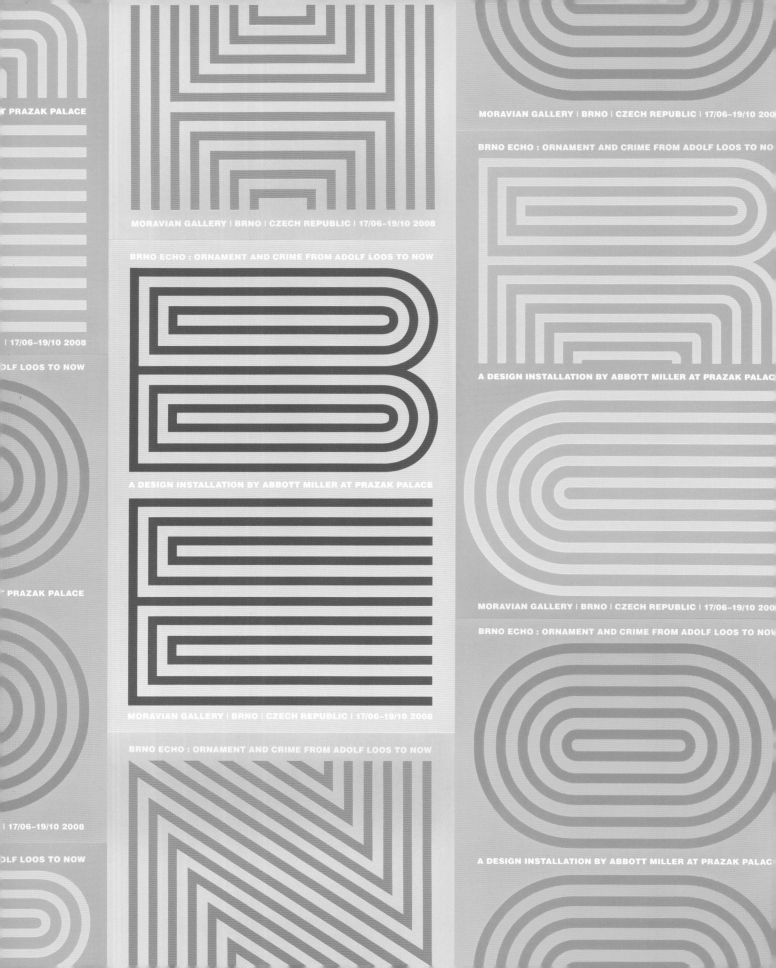

MORAVIAN GALLERY | BRNO | CZECH REPUBLIC | 17/06–19/10 2008

BRNO ECHO : ORNAMENT AND CRIME FROM ADOLF LOOS TO NOW

A DESIGN INSTALLATION BY ABBOTT MILLER AT PRAZAK PALACE

MORAVIAN GALLERY | BRNO | CZECH REPUBLIC | 17/06–19/10 2008

RNO ECHO : ORNAMENT AND CRIME FROM ADOLF LOOS TO NOW

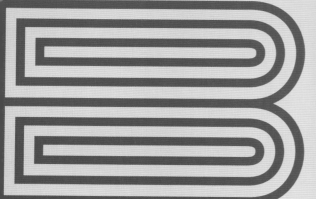

A DESIGN INSTALLATION BY ABBOTT MILLER AT PRAZAK PALACE

MORAVIAN GALLERY | BRNO | CZECH REPUBLIC | 17/06–19/10 2008

BRNO ECHO : ORNAMENT AND CRIME FROM ADOLF LOOS TO NOW

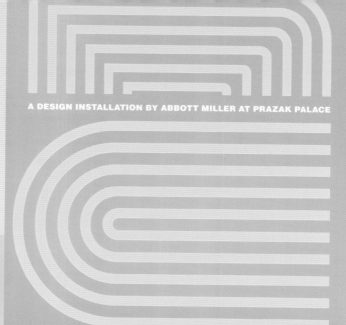

MORAVIAN GALLERY | BRNO | CZECH REPUBLIC | 17/06–19/10 2008

BRNO ECHO : ORNAMENT AND CRIME FROM ADOLF LOOS TO NOW

A DESIGN INSTALLATION BY ABBOTT MILLER AT PRAZAK PALACE

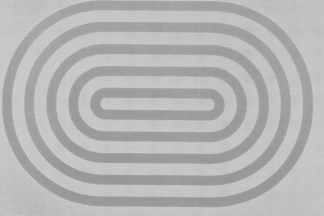

MORAVIAN GALLERY | BRNO | CZECH REPUBLIC | 17/06–19/10 2008

BRNO ECHO : ORNAMENT AND CRIME FROM ADOLF LOOS TO NOW

MORAVIAN GALL

BRNO ECHO : OR

A DESIGN INSTAM

MORAVIAN GALLE

BRNO ECHO : ORI

The publication for *Brno Echo* used facing pages to juxtapose historic and contemporary design. In the middle row, left, a 2002 chair by the Campagna Brothers is shown opposite a 1910 drawing for a textile by Otto Czeschka.

The wall texts throughout the show revealed a frustration with the "humiliated repetition" (Roland Barthes) of contemporary life, set against the joyful profusion of forms and colors in the galleries.

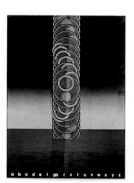

"The bastard form of mass culture is
humiliated repetition... always new books,
new programs, new films, news items,
but always the same meaning."

Roland Barthes, *The Pleasure of the Text*, 1975

the globe is all one, anybody can hear
everything and everybody can hear the same
thing, so what is the use of conquering?"

Gertrude Stein, *Wars I Have Seen*, 1943

FLOCK MOVEMENT
This diagram describes the field of vision of a simulated bird. The artificial bird responds to other birds that fall inside its field of vision. The bird is attracted to its flock mates but is also repelled from them. These rules allow for the cohesion of the flock while preventing collision.

Any given bird has its own circle of vision; the bird is influenced by others that fall within its circle. The same bird occupies the edge of other birds' circles, allowing it to influence them. In this installation, a "leader flock" is one that influences others but is not influenced by them, owing to its visual position. The leader flock does not have a command role, however. If the flock were to change direction, a new bird would overtake the lead. Uroš Leko Bajec, Nikolaj Zimic, and Mika Mraz, 2005.

LEADER FLOCK

LEADER

STRAGGLER

LEADERLESS FLOCK

STRAGGLER

Social insects build their worlds as a matter of course.[1] They follow no directions from a king, queen, or architect, but engage in a collective process in which millions of independent actions ultimately yield a larger order. Social insects exchange simple signals that either attract or repel their fellow colonists, or activate or inhibit a mechanical or biological action. Many ant species lay down a pheromone trail as they travel; when a useful food source is identified, the larger number of ants traveling in that direction produce a stronger trail that induces more ants to follow. Foraging ants initially scurry about in a random fashion, but will eventually establish a common direction.

The movement of a flock of birds, a school of fish, or a herd of sheep results from local communications among nearest neighbors. A pioneering attempt to simulate the mass movement of birds was conducted by the computer animator Craig Reynolds in the mid-1980s. Reynolds's digital birds — which he called "boids" — obey a simple set of rules: match the speed and direction (velocity) of your neighbor, avoid colliding with your neighbor, and try to get to the center of the group. The center-seeking tendency keeps the boids together, while the no-bumping rule prevents them from piling up at the same spot. As an animator, Reynolds succeeded in reproducing not just the motion of an individual bird, but the overall behavior of the group.[2]

3 Jean-Louis Deneubourg, Guy Theraulaz, and Ralph Beckers, "Swarm-Made Architectures," First European Conference in Artificial Life (Paris, 1991): 18–38.
4 Craig C. Reynolds, "Flocks, Herds, and Schools: A Distributed Behavioral Model," Computer Graphics 21, no. 4 (1987): 25–34.
5 On the political ambivalence of the swarm, see Eugene Thacker, "Networks, Swarms, Multitudes, Part One," http://www.ctheory.net/text_file?pick=27, ed. Arthur and Marilouise Kroker.

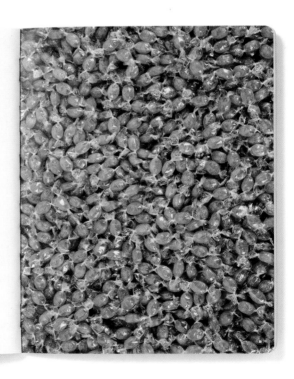

ORDER

ARMY
ants foraging together in a line

ARMY
organized armed land force

SWARM
a group of bees leaving with their queen to create a new colony; or army ants foraging for food

SOCIETY
group of organisms living together within a structured system

DROVE
flock or sheep moving together

FLOCK
birds or sheep moving together as a group

FLOCK
Christian congregation

HERD
group of people sharing an action or mentality

HERD
domestic animals living in a group, especially cattle, sheep, or goats

DROVE
crowd moving together

SWARM
large group of people, human, or society, a swarm of bees

ANIMAL — HUMAN

MOB
disorderly crowd

CROWD
large gathering of people

PACK
animals hunting together; a pack of wolves

PACK
loosely organized net of cohorts; a gang

RIOT
disturbance of the peace or uncontrolled rowdiness by a crowd

MOB
lone predators attacking together opportunistically; mobbing sharks

DISORDER

LONE WOLF

SWARM MAP
Honeybee swarms are complex but directed, while a swarm of flies gathers for no social purpose, drawn together only by a common attraction to sugar or decay. To confront the biopolitical diversity of the swarm, we created this semantic map. The map is organized around two axes: ORDER/DISORDER and ANIMAL/HUMAN. The flow of concepts across these categories endows swarms with their beauty and terror. Consider the territory occupied by the word swarm. On the one hand, swarm refers to the highly specific behavior of honeybees as they divide their "colony and relocate, or to the dramatic fancy of tropical army ants as they fan across the forest floor relentlessly poisoning their prey. But swarming also descends into disorder.

The crowd is a concept that cuts across numerous modes of human assembly, many of them paralleled in the world of animals. When we refer to people as a herd, we speak of a crowd that thinks alike — a populace as docile as a bunch of sheep. A drove is a group of creatures pushed in a single direction by a dog, a shepherd, or a great sale at Barney's. Riots and mobs, on the other hand, embody the capacity of the crowd to wreak violence and destruction. Sharks are said to mob around their prey in an opportunistic way, not to achieve a common goal but to seize upon the weakness of the victims.

FELIX GONZALEZ-TORRES
"Untitled" (Rossmore II), 1991
Green candies individually wrapped in cellophane, endless supply. Overall dimensions vary with installation. Ideal weight: 75 lb.
Installation view: "Felix Gonzalez-Torres,"
Serpentine Gallery, London, 2000
© The Felix Gonzalez-Torres Foundation
Courtesy of Andrea Rosen Gallery, New York, and Serpentine Gallery, London
Photo: Stephen White
Detail Photo: Oren Slor

Spreads from *Swarm*, featuring information graphics that analyze swarming in animal and human communities, and a sculpture by Felix Gonzalez-Torres. A view of the installation shows chairs by the Campana Brothers and paintings by Trenton Doyle Hancock.

swarm

Contemporary art, science, design, digital media, and social theory have analyzed decentralized and unplanned modes of organization under the rubric of swarm theory. *Swarm* (2005) was an exhibition and publication I curated and designed with Ellen Lupton for the Fabric Workshop and Museum in Philadelphia. The project presented works by artists and designers influenced by the theoretical and visual effects of swarming, linking practices that aggregate masses of objects, images, data, and organisms.

A few artists—Paul Pfeiffer, Yanagi Yukinori, and Peter Kogler—incorporate the images and behavior of insects. *Swarm* connected the social life of bees, birds, crowds, and cities to contemporary aesthetics, as seen in the fascination with how simple, discrete units accumulate into complex systems.

The catalog is modeled on a naturalist field guide and features information graphics of swarms occurring in the human and animal worlds—from army ants and honeybees to traffic and suburban sprawl.

design for a living world

The Nature Conservancy commissioned us to create a project about design and conservation. The goal was to expand awareness of its mission by highlighting the conservancy's work in communities around the globe. Our concept was to commission ten designers from the fields of fashion, product, and industrial design to work with sustainably grown and harvested materials from endangered ecosystems. Scientists at the conservancy identified provocative regions and materials, and we selected designers with natural affinities for the different materials. *Design for a Living World* (2009) highlighted conservation and land management, as well as effectively showed how designers are inspired by materials. A critical part of the project was the documentary photography of Ami Vitale, who spent nearly a year traveling to each region, providing a powerful visual thread connecting our design of the exhibition, book, and website.

Cover and spreads from
Design for a Living World, 2009

CHICLE LATEX   125

hella jongerius

Hella Jongerius, known for her unusual use of materials and her interest in mixing craft processes with advanced industrial techniques, is among the world's leading experimental designers. Based in Rotterdam, Jongerius has been creating influential designs for textiles, furniture, vessels, and other objects since the early 1990s. She is a leading voice within the distinctive design community of the Netherlands, stimulating a global discourse on materials, functionality, and production. Her studio, Jongeriuslab, creates short-run, one-of-a-kind experimental works as well as objects for mass production.

Jongerius often combines diverse elements and techniques to create overtly collaged products, such as ceramic vases with stitching and perforation, as well as sofas upholstered in shifting colors of wool. Her Long Neck and Groove vases combine parts cut from existing vessels and bound together with tape. Jongerius's Pushed Soft Washtub, a bathroom fixture made from flexible polyurethane, places a resilient material into a domestic space where cold, hard surfaces are expected.

Conservation functions as both medium and metaphor across Jongerius's work, as she has sought to reuse abandoned materials as well as recombine existing textile patterns or bring new energy to traditional craft practices. In place of the seamless sameness favored by mass production, she seeks out variation, imperfection, and change. Many pieces suggest a process of coming undone as much as a process of completion.

The Nature Conservancy partnered with Jongerius to explore the potential of chicle latex, a substance never before used in product design. She approached this daunting task with the open mind of a scientist and explorer, investigating its adhesive properties and molding characteristics. As a complement to Jongerius's chicle project, Glee Gum—one of today's leading makers of organic, chicle-based chewing gum, based in Providence, Rhode Island—is creating a *Design for a Living World* gum flavored with cardamom and honey from the Yucatán.

Dutch designer Hella Jongerius stretches chicle latex in her studio in Rotterdam as she experiments with the material's practical uses.

In its raw state, chicle latex is a milky-white liquid. To transform it into a usable material, the chicleros of the ejido Veinte de Noviembre heat it

When the dried bricks of chicle latex arrived at Hella Jongerius's studio in the Netherlands, she began exploring the design potential of a product

Jongerius discovered that chicle heated at lower temperatures yielded a viscous substance that made an excellent adhesive and could be w

53

Our exhibition design was adaptable to different locations and architectural settings. Our first venue, the Cooper-Hewitt, National Design Museum, is a landmarked interior, which engendered a delicate approach that avoided invasive connections and required a minimal footprint.

Photographs and texts were printed directly on recycled aluminum panels, which avoided paper or vinyl substrates.

The display vitrines were based on mobile and lightweight furniture typologies. Lighting was integrated in a bar that formed a ribbon around the top of the display case.

The following page shows a detail of Hella Jongerius's project using chicle latex in Mexico.

A gallery dedicated to designer Ted Muehling's project in Micronesia, which used vegetable ivory and black pearls, created the feel of an underwater chamber.

A view of designer Yves Behar's project with a women's chocolate cooperative in Costa Rica shows how the wall armatures and shingles create multilayered photographic collages.

The use of sustainable materials was integrated throughout the exhibition. The wall structures and casework were made of FSC-certified Spanish Cedar harvested from Bolivia. The decks of the cases were made of Medite II, a medium-density fiberboard manufactured from 100 percent recycled or recovered wood fibers that are bonded with formaldehyde-free resin.

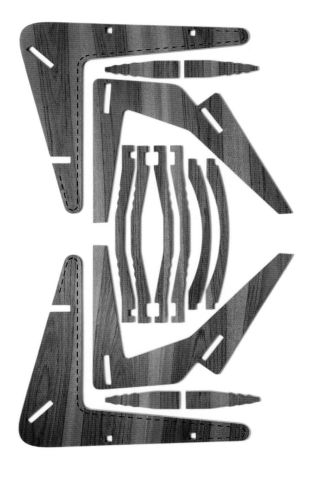

As one of the designers in the exhibition, I created a chair made of FSC-certified plywood produced in Bolivia. I traveled to Bolivia with a designer on my team, Brian Raby, and we observed traditional furniture making, as well as CNC-milling. Our design yields three chairs from a single sheet of plywood. The elements are shipped flat and assembled without glue. The back and seat are formed by a continuous cotton tape—similar to that used in Amish furniture—that is woven through slots cut along the edge of the frame.

the only way to do it is to do it

The magazine *Dance Ink* (1991–96) was an early laboratory where I learned how to work with photography and collaborate with photographers. Our small budget and even smaller circulation afforded us enormous freedom. I had never designed a magazine before and was given the opportunity to find my way through it. In the course of working on *Dance Ink* I came across a quote from Merce Cunningham: "The only way to do it is to do it," which perfectly summarized my experience. I didn't know what I didn't know, and felt free of the constraints that come with a more "sophisticated" understanding of magazine design. We published quarterly and developed an intense community of readers, gaining different audiences that were drawn to its writing, photography, and design.

Early on we realized that most of our audience subscribed to the magazine—only a fraction of our issues were sold on the newsstand—giving us license to be less consistent with our identity and more experimental. We even pushed the word *Dance* to the back cover so that only *Ink* remained on the front. Typographically I started off with an allegiance to Martin Majoor's then-new typeface Scala, but I soon realized that *Dance Ink* could be a broader playground for experimentation with design and production.

From the earliest issues, I used duotone printing, metallic ink, and varied paper stocks, rethinking the craft of the whole production with each issue. I was fascinated by the nuance and variety of different black-plus-color duotone combinations. While our black-and-white printing was initially a response to a tight budget, it came to substantially shape the visual spirit of the magazine and made it stand out. When I look back at these issues, their lack of four-color photography gives them a pleasantly confusing relationship to time.

Dance Ink: Photographs, 1997

A range of covers reveal a playful approach to the magazine's identity, ranging from the wrap-around treatment for Diana Ross and the Supremes (1994), to a mysterious cover featuring a painting by Mark Tansey (1995). Esther Williams is lowered into water against a dotted version of *Ink* (1995), and Fred Astaire and Hermes Pan dance under a simple sans serif iteration (1996).

DIAMANDA GALÁS

Has been called a witch and an anti-christ in the Italian media. The truth is she is a forty-one-year-old composer, activist, musician, writer, performance artist, and outspoken health activist who uses an extraordinary range of amplified sounds – spoken, sung, and shrieked – to illustrate the mental and physical suffering of people with AIDS. Her work is definitely not easy listening.

Galás's activism extends beyond the stage. As a member of the AIDS Coalition to Unleash Power (ACT UP), she was arrested four years ago at St. Patrick's Cathedral during a demonstration protesting John Cardinal O'Connor's position on women's reproductive rights and his interference in the teaching of safe-sex practices in New York City public schools. Galás has also spent time playing the piano for bedridden AIDS patients at the V.A. Medical Center.

On the fingers of her left hand are tattooed the words WE ARE ALL HIV+; her brother died from AIDS-related illnesses in 1986.

During her recent Insekta, a piece about mental disintegration that premiered at Lincoln Center last July, Galás spent most of the performance trapped in a huge cage suspended above the stage. In her earlier Plague Mass, which she will tour this fall, Galás uses biblical texts, often babbled in Greek and Latin, to condemn the religious hypocrisy that has hampered the fight against AIDS. ◆ WILLIAM HARRIS   PHOTOGRAPHS: JOANNE SAVIO

PLAGUE MASS *ILLUSTRATES THE SPECTATOR SPORT OF TORTURE. JUST AS ANCIENT ROMANS FLOCKED TO THE COLOSSEUM TO SEE PEOPLE TORTURED, AIDS HAS BECOME A SPECTATOR SPORT FOR MANY AMERICANS. THEY SEEM TO ENJOY WATCHING GAY MEN, PEOPLE OF COLOR, AND IV-DRUG USERS DIE.*

I SEE THE AIDS EPIDEMIC AS A KIND OF GERM WARFARE, AND ITS RESOLUTION HAS BEEN APPROACHED THAT WAY, TOO. OTHERWISE IT WOULDN'T BE SO COMPLETELY OUT OF CONTROL. I CAN ALSO GUARANTEE THAT FOR EVERY PERSON LIKE MYSELF WHO SAYS SOMETHING LIKE THIS, THERE ARE GOING TO BE NINETY-NINE OTHER PEOPLE WHO SAY, "CALM DOWN, THERE'S NO PROOF." WELL, THERE'S NO PROOF EITHER WAY. THEY HAVE NO MORE PROOF THAN I DO.

BILLIONS OF DOLLARS ARE SPENT ON MILITARY RESEARCH, BUT ONLY A FRACTION OF THAT AMOUNT IS PUT TOWARD EXISTING DISEASES IN THE POPULATION. IT'S NAIVE TO ASSUME THAT A LOT OF VIRUSES WE ARE NOW DEALING WITH HAVEN'T BEEN INTRODUCED BY CHANCE OR NEGLECT. SCIENCE INCLUDES BOTH. ◆ DIAMANDA GALÁS

A 1993 issue includes a feature on performance artist Diamanda Galás addressing the AIDS epidemic. In a 1995 issue Nancy Dalva analyzes the almost surgical cuts in clothing by Geoffrey Beene, with a diagrammatic overlay on vellum. A 1995 issue includes a group portrait by Timothy Greenfield-Sanders of the performers in playright John Jesurun's *Chang in a Void Moon.* Characters are identified with different symbols and letterforms on both sides of a vellum sheet. The cast includes Frank Maya, John Kelly, David Cale, and Steve Buscemi.

Second Skin
NANCY DALVA DISSECTS GEOFFREY BEENE

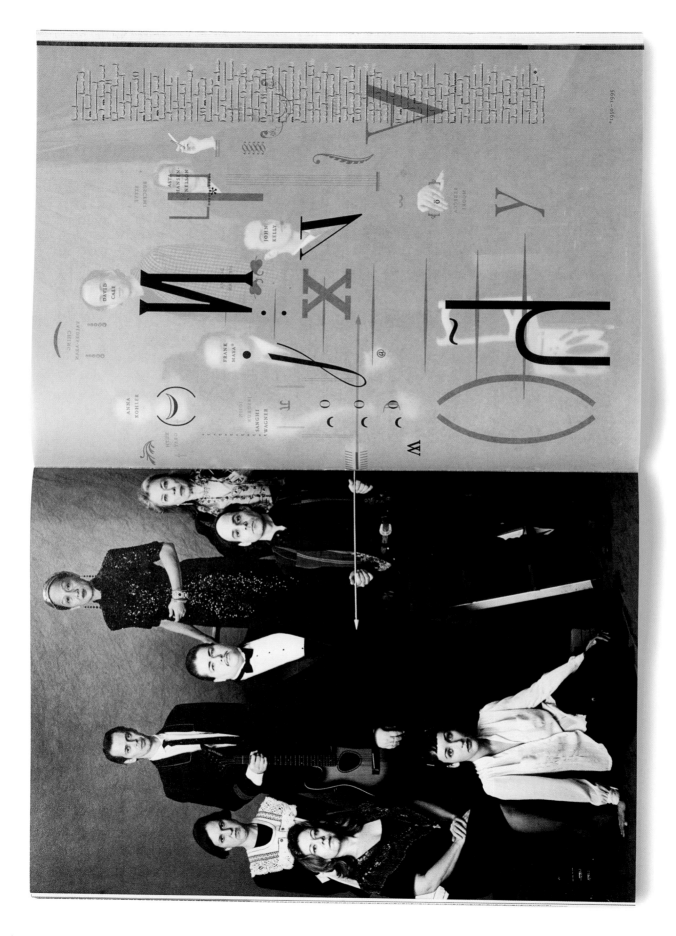

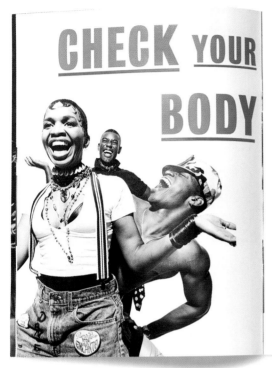

CHECK YOUR BODY

AT THE DOOR

BODY

If you have committed your life to dancing—
spending up to thirty hours a week perfecting your technique and
style—and if you have risen to the top in your discipline,
then it must be acknowledged that you are an artist. In the world
of club dancing—where style is everything—Archie Burnett,
Barbara Tucker, Willi Ninja, and Brahms La Fortune are hailed as **prime movers.**

Now in their early thirties, they began dancing as children, and except for Burnett, started clubbing at about thirteen years old. None has taken a conventional class. Instead, they absorbed dance informally, picking up steps and attitudes from television, taking moves from the street or other dancers around Manhattan.

Club dancing flourishes in the dark, driven by deep bass sounds that vibrate the sternum. Certain bass tones, carefully engineered in the studio for amplification by giant 909 and 808 speakers, are "created so you don't hear you feel them," La Fortune explains. "It is intentional—the equivalent of your heart on the outside of your body." The club provides a synthetic environment of sound and motion, where the only illumination is stabbing shafts of light that briefly reveal a dancer, a gesture, a circle of freestyling improvisers battling one another with their best moves. The darkness, the music, and the dense, layered motion create another reality. Packed in the crowd, an individual can become anonymous, liberated, free to experiment.

In quick improvisational exchanges, dance motions are born from a cross-blending of ethnic, gender, regional, and even neighborhood styles. Humor and commentary are embedded in this process—as in this optimistic premise: that dance is always in evolution, and that reinvention and adaptability are strategies for what life, at its best, should be.

From the outside, an underground club is unremarkable: a black door with no sign, no address. Around eleven p.m. the early clubgoers show up, and by one in the morning clots of people are bunched before the entrance, kept at bay by bouncers and the doormen.

Willi Ninja is one of these gatekeepers, always dressed in an extravagant outfit. For him, being a doorman is a test of patience and endurance. For those who want to get in, Ninja's nod of acceptance is a recognition of how they fit in to an intricate hierarchy: the great dancers, the industry types, the regulars. Although the clubs are not private, they shun publicity. Only the initiated know where they are located, which night is the right one for dancing, which is the right door.

One look tells you that Archie Burnett is a serious dancer. No flash: baseball cap, black leather jacket, Levis, sneakers. But because he is six feet, four inches tall, with a carefully sculpted body, a deep voice, and easy confidence, he has presence. And because he and Ninja have known each other for years, and Burnett is one of the most respected dancers, he enters immediately.

"Underground clubs specialize in anonymity," Burnett says. "For the real diehards, that is where they go, when they go. When you enter a place like that, you must go through a rite of passage—commonly called 'getting frisked.' The reason is that you have to give of yourself in order to get. You must give up your personal being to this particular space so that once inside, you can experience what the club has to offer. It is also an affirmation of 'I come in peace.'

> "As you walk in, you hear and smell the sounds,
> which get your blood pumping and adrenaline flowing.
> The club itself is a mood changer. You may have
> had the worst day, but when you are in there for two
> hours, your mood will change. It's about music,
> energy, spirituality, all in one. But you must
> give yourself over to it. You have no choice because
> the DJ is going to make you work."

Once inside, Burnett steps onto the floor, testing the music with small slipping steps that carve out a minuscule personal stage. He focuses down on his feet, dipping in a quick turn to avoid a collision, never raising his head, listening intently to the beat. Constantly in motion, he scans the music for a rhythm to ride. Once he finds it, he moves out with big gestures, arms twirling around his body in figure eights that suddenly snap into millisecond freezes. As he breaks into a sweat, he strips down to black bicycle tights. A consummate freestyler, he deftly combines voguing, whacking, pantomime, and lofting pull dives and splits to the floor mixed with kung fu and gymnastics.

Text: Sally Sommer Photographs: Andrew Eccles

Facing page (from left to right): Barbara Tucker, Brahms La Fortune, Archie Burnett
above: La Fortune

left: Tucker, La Fortune, above: Burnett

A 1994 issue includes a story
about club dancing and voguing,
featuring photographs of
Barbara Tucker, Brahms La Fortune,
Archie Burnett, and Willi Ninja.
An image of Prince by Herb Ritts
mirrors itself. Choreographer
Jonathan Burrows is documented
in photographs by Josef Astor.
The cover was photographed by
Joanne Savio, from an exhibition of
the couturier Charles James.

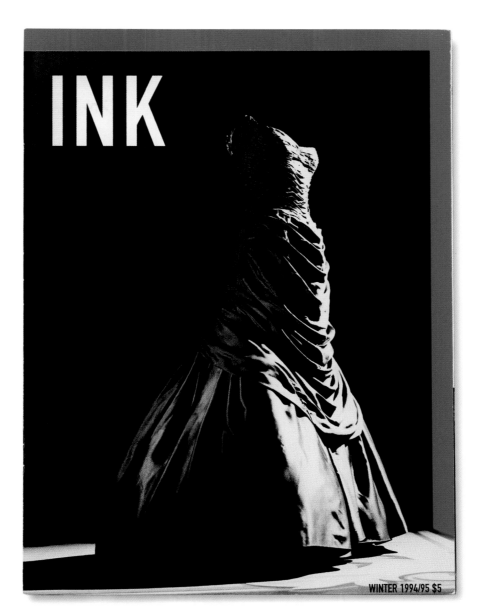

INK

WINTER 1994/95 $5

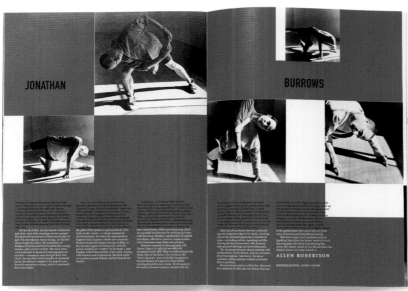

JONATHAN

BURROWS

ALLEN ROBERTSON

PHOTOGRAPHS, JOSEF ASTOR

A 1995 issue uses rough, colored paper and large type to create a distinctive look inspired by newspapers and tabloids. An essay on a Dario Argento horror film called *Suspiria* — set in a ballet academy run by a coven — considers the tradition of evil in classical ballet.

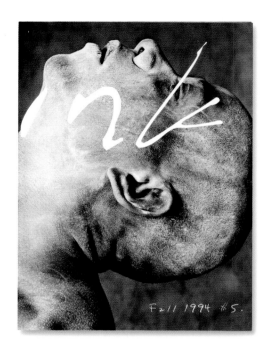

A 1994 issue uses a larger format, 10.5 by 14 inches, with a poster-like approach to its pages. Choreographer Ralph Lemon, dusted in powder, was photographed by Andrew Eccles.

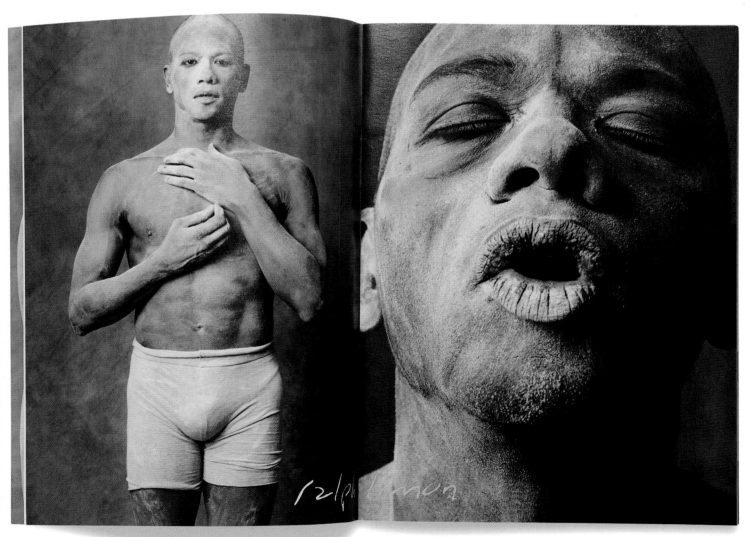

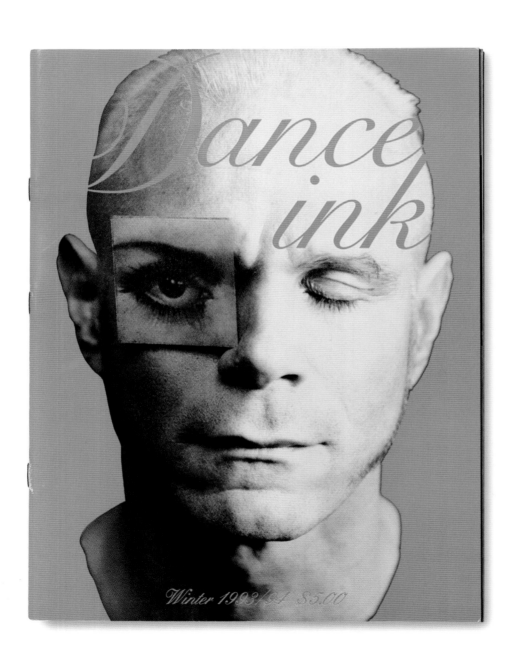

A characteristically eclectic
1993 issue includes a piece on
Helmut Newton, an essay
on rodeos with images by Arthur
Elgort, photographs of dancer
Lance Gries by Stewart Shining,
an essay on Eadweard Muybridge,
and a cover portrait of artist
Charles Atlas by Josef Astor. The
issue explores all the things you
can do with black, fluorescent
orange, and warm gray: surprinting,
reversing, and floods of ink.

Performer-choreogra
Lance G

softens the cor

s session
photographer
art Shining,

eeps an edge.

Stacy Caddell

Jamie Bishton

Margo Fdfe

Robert LaFosse

fréde

A 1996 issue focuses exclusively on dancers and choreographers: New York City Ballet soloist Ethan Stiefel was photographed by Guzman; dancers Frédéric Gafner and Peter Boal performed for photographer Andrew Eccles; and the Bonsai Group, an ensemble of dancers—Lance Gries, Jodi Melnick, Jamie Bishton, Robert LaFosse, Kevin O'Day, and Stacy Caddell—were photographed by Ruven Afanador.

Summer 1996 $5

ink

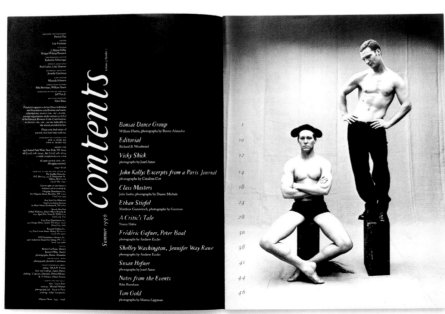

EDITOR IN CHIEF/PUBLISHER
Patricia Tyse

EDITOR
Lise Friedman

ASSISTANT EDITOR
J. Abbott Miller

PHOTOGRAPHY EDITOR
Katherine Schlesinger

SENIOR EDITORS
Paul Carter, Luke Hayman

EDITORIAL ASSISTANTS
Jennifer Cutshman

COPY EDITOR
Miranda Schwartz

INTERNS
Riko Bertram, William Harris

SUBSCRIPTION AND CIRCULATION
Jeff Tyse, Jr.

DANCE INK BOARD
Ellen Bates

contents

Volume 7 Number 2

Summer 1996

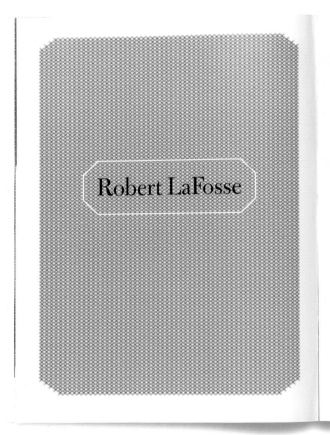

Robert LaFosse

ELEVEN

pilar
rioja

A 1995 issue dispenses with almost all text, relying on photography and ornamental patterning. Robert LaFosse was photographed in a kilt by Andrew Eccles. Rob Besserer performed a deranged *Swan Lake* duet with a (fake) swan for Duane Michals. Flamenco dance legend Pilar Rioja ruffled and stomped for K. C. Bailey.

design is a measure of energy

Formal and deliberate, his voice had a southern, Truman Capote drawl. His hair was snowy white and his eyes were framed with large black glasses. The studio was hushed and reverential: I had already been warned to call him "Mr. Beene," but still I was not prepared for the rarified atmosphere I encountered. Geoffrey Beene was—like his favorite flower, a hothouse orchid—sustained by an elaborate support mechanism, yielding bursts of beauty as long as the hushed decorum of the studio was maintained.

I was mystified by the nature of our first meeting, but about a month later he asked if I would design one of his shows. He was frustrated by typical runway presentations, because he thought they failed to accurately show the clothing. Instead, he wanted to create a daylong exhibition with clothing shown on dress forms, allowing people to see the craft and detail. His refusal to play by the rules defined his career: he derived clarity and focus in his work by defining himself as an outsider to the preoccupations of the fashion industry. He could get swept up in pronouncements about the cynicism and ignorance of fashion, but then just as quickly start to rhapsodize about a button or a seam or a fabric that had caught his eye.

One of his many sayings was "design is a measure of energy," which conveys the sense of design as a distillation of complex forces, insight, and sustained attention.

He evolved his own lexicon, captured in shorthand phrases: "saints and sinners" (dresses that present a chaste image in the front with an unexpectedly revealing back), "new erogenous zones" (his emphasis on areas like the small of the back, or the collarbone or shoulder blades); and "geometry" (by which he meant triangles, a primary shape recurring in his work). His attitude about design was cosmopolitan, synthesizing influences from Japanese design, the Wiener Werkstätte, the Bauhaus, African textiles, and in a series of early appropriations, Pop Art and the vernacular of cartoons, football jerseys, and traffic signs. His work offered a rare combination of being both very cerebral and totally sensual.

I was privileged to have had a total immersion in his work: over the course of a decade I designed many of his shows on runways and in galleries, a retrospective, books, and graphics. Our friendship was close but formal, more like a student and teacher. Over the years I worked with him, his work and passion for independent design thinking made him a hero to those around him.

Geoffrey Beene, 1999.
Photograph by Christian Witkin

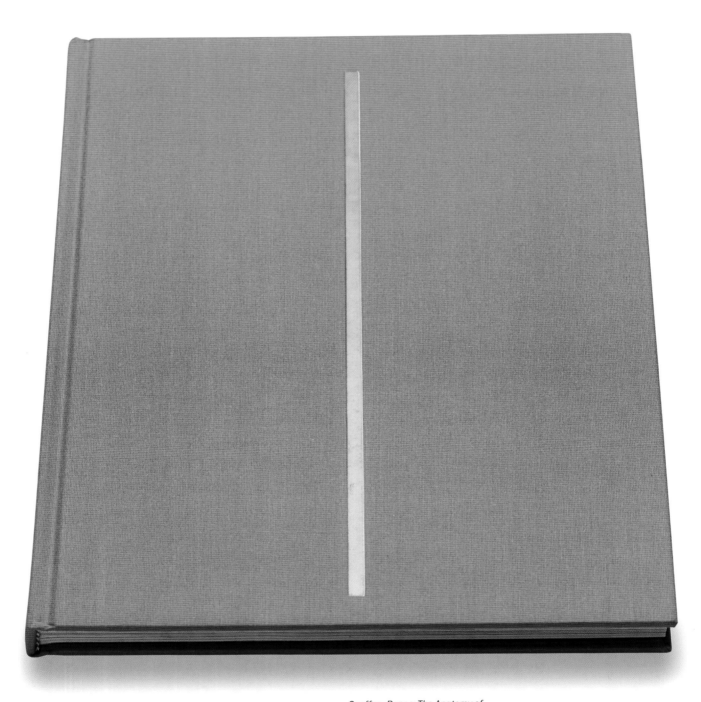

Geoffrey Beene: The Anatomy of His Work (1995) made diverse styles of photography coherent through layouts with generous white space. My favorite moment shows a figure moving across the spread, partially hidden within the depth of the binding.

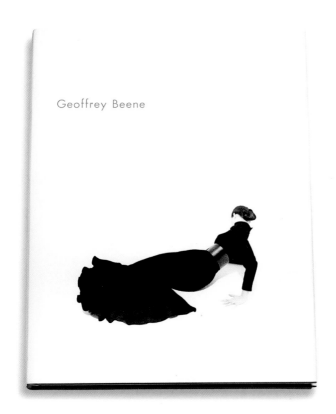

Geoffrey Beene

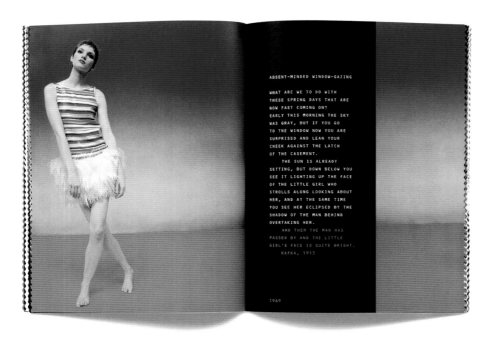

ABSENT-MINDED WINDOW-GAZING

WHAT ARE WE TO DO WITH
THESE SPRING DAYS THAT ARE
NOW FAST COMING ON?
EARLY THIS MORNING THE SKY
WAS GRAY, BUT IF YOU GO
TO THE WINDOW NOW YOU ARE
SURPRISED AND LEAN YOUR
CHEEK AGAINST THE LATCH
OF THE CASEMENT.
    THE SUN IS ALREADY
SETTING, BUT DOWN BELOW YOU
SEE IT LIGHTING UP THE FACE
OF THE LITTLE GIRL WHO
STROLLS ALONG LOOKING ABOUT
HER, AND AT THE SAME TIME
YOU SEE HER ECLIPSED BY THE
SHADOW OF THE MAN BEHIND
OVERTAKING HER.
    AND THEN THE MAN HAS
PASSED BY AND THE LITTLE
GIRL'S FACE IS QUITE BRIGHT.
KAFKA, 1913

1969

I designed and produced a book to accompany Unbound (1994), a Geoffrey Beene retrospective at the Museum of the Fashion Institute of Technology. Photographs by Josef Astor were shot with saturated colored backgrounds. A pinking-sheared edge on the pages creates an immediate association between paper and fabric. A series of enigmatic short stories by Franz Kafka, in which clothing plays a central role, act as a counterpoint to the photographs.

The posters use the make-ready sheets for the book, unified by a silkscreened layer of orange text. The posters were wheat-pasted on the street and within the tall entrance, accompanied by a figure atop a ladder completing the installation.

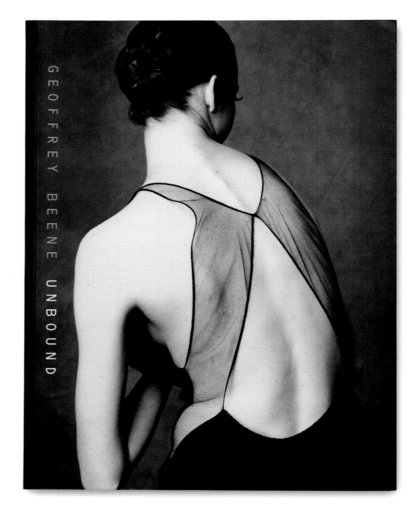

GEOFFREY BEENE UNBOUND

THE MUSEUM AT F.I.T
SEVENTH AVE AT 27TH
NEW YORK / NEW YORK

GEOFFREY
BEENE
UNBOUND

FEB. 16 — APR. 30
TUE-FRI NOON TO 8
SATURDAYS 10 TO 5

Unbound was staged in a large central gallery accessed from both directions through two symmetrical doors at each end. I designed two pairs of staircases that spanned the entire length of the space. The elevation of the stairs created sight lines to the clothes when the galleries were full, activating an otherwise dormant zone of the high-ceilinged space.

A video projection—a collaboration with the artist Judith Barry—features a figure emerging from darkness: walking forward, she briefly disappears as she reaches her largest scale at the end of the gallery. After a slight delay—allowing for the time it would take in real time—she reappears as a mirage, captured on a veil hung in the middle of the space. After intersecting the veil, she reappears, seen from the back, on the opposite wall. Eight different figures drift through the space in fifteen minute intervals.

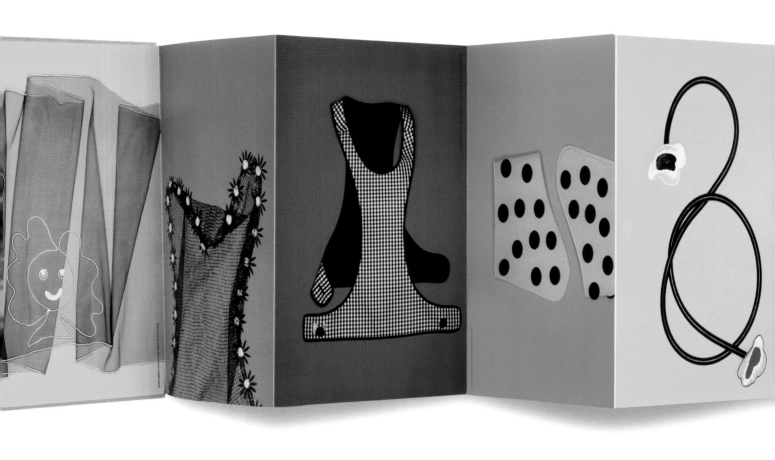

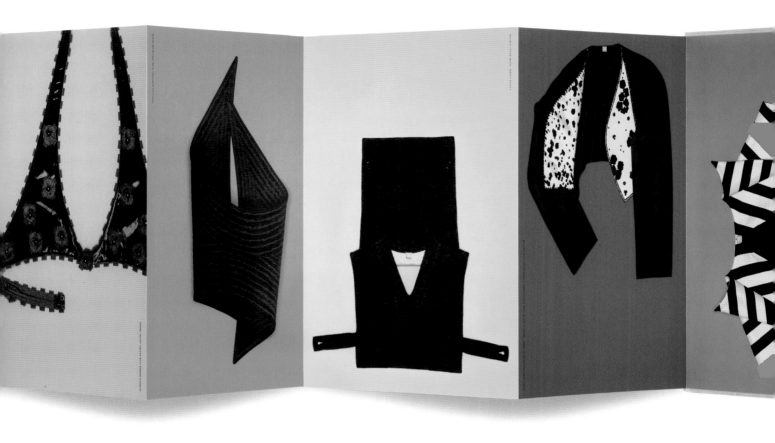

Geoffrey Beene: A Design Tribute (2005) celebrates the designer's legacy, focusing on his inspiration from dance and inventive use of materials. The book was fabricated as a trio of accordion-bound documents within a slipcase. One side features details of accessories photographed by Jay Zukerkorn. The reverse side shows dancer Holley Farmer in photographs by Shoji van Kazumi. The publication includes essays by Patricia Tarr, Nancy Dalva, and myself.

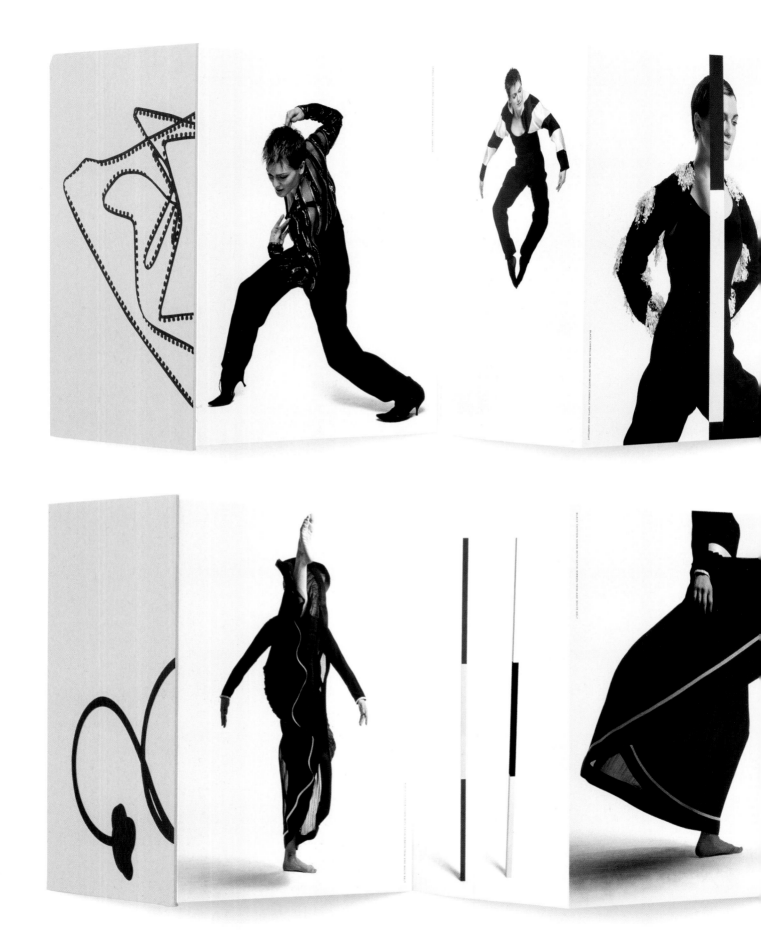

This publication is our tribut[e]
Geoffrey Beene, the late, gre[at]
of the twentieth century and a[n]
esteemed member of the 2wi[ce]
Advisory Panel. In the latter [...]
Mr. Beene inspired us with his [...]
and enthusiasm for our work. [...]
former, he made designs so m[...]
that we included them in alm[ost]
issue of 2wice magazine.

I came to know Mr. Beene as [...]
his customers. Sometime afte[r]
daughter's birth in 1979, I sp[...]
on a Geoffrey Beene dress, he [...]
of a sophisticated sundress. T[...]
garment—so comfortable, so [...]
so versatile—was the beginni[ng]
25-year addiction. Like many [...]
I suppose, it crept up on me sl[...]
I never intended to wear only [...]
Beene clothes; in fact, I still p[...]
things by other designers with [...]
intention of wearing them. But [...]
again, with my husband dresse[d]
some event and patiently wait[ing]
race to the closet and change i[nto]
beloved Beene. Eventually, I s[...]
wearing anything else.

The relationship between a wo[man]
her wardrobe is curious. Some [...]
shop for clothes that flatter th[...]
them. Some women shop for clo[thes]
the moment, dressing in the cu[rrent]
style regardless of its merits. B[...]
groups share the conviction th[at]
clothes should serve them, eit[her]
enhancing their appearance or [...]
them the happiness of wearing [...]
the-minute style. Beene cloth[es]
utterly different. They could b[e]
upon to fit exquisitely, but th[...]
tency of the vision meant that [...]
changed only in subtle ways fr[om]
to year. No part of a Beene war[...]
ever out of style: indeed, subse[...]
purchases simply revealed his [...]
more depth. And of course ther[e]
the originality, the wit, the mate[...]
the lightness. There could be n[...]
about it: these clothes were ma[...]
and unusual and rare. In no tim[e]
I changed from a woman who w[...]
clothes to serve her into a wom[an]
served her clothes. And so bega[n]
years of collecting Beene, acqui[...]

One of my earliest proje[ct]
was as art director of a m[...]
Dance Ink, published by [...]
The magazine had a small [...]
following, and among the [...]
was Geoffrey Beene. Pat[...]
introduced Mr. Beene to [...]
and he was so enthusiast[ic]
that he invited us to his s[...]

Shortly afterwards, he ca[...]
I would design an exhibi[tion]
The loyalty and commitm[ent]
in this first collaboratio[n]
our friendship from that [...]
For over a decade I worke[d]
on books, exhibitions, ad[...]
the presentation of many [...]
tions on stage.

Mr. Beene's work was a c[...]
investigation of opposit[es]
explored endlessly and in[...]
It was work and play, ser[ious]
funny, front and back, ab[...]
figurative. Throughout, h[...]
satisfying himself above [...]
work was immediate pro[...]
offered by another of the [...]
great designers, Charles [...]
"Take your pleasures seri[ously]
Beene's pleasures could f[...]
a seductive piece of fabr[ic]
collar meets the neck, or [...]
to himself—and his work[...]
structing a garment with [...]
that spirals around the b[ody]
were the relationship bet[ween]
and modernity, sensuali[ty]
austerity and luxury.

While he was revered as a [...]
with a towering reputatio[n]
funny, loquacious, and in[...]
a fantastic way of telling [...]
stories, and he loved pun[...]
phrase. Around the time [...]
working with him in 199[...]
if disclosing something [...]
learn irrefutably—"Oran[ge]
red." Orange had long b[een]
color, but now I could de[...]
declaration of authority.

When I designed Mr. Bee[ne]
tive at the Museum of th[e]
Institute of Technology. [...]
I could record some of ou[r]

a white cube is a black box

2wice was conceived as a biannual publication poised at the intersection of the visual and performing arts: a white cube in which to display art and a black box performance space for collaborations with performers and photographers. The editorial perspective is united by idiosyncratic themes that provide a starting point for essays and art direction. As editor and designer, I have been able to develop both its editorial content and its visual expression. When we published the first issue in 1997, *2wice* was an exotic entry in the world of magazines, hearkening back to art- and design-driven publications of the past such as *Flair*, *FMR*, and *Portfolio*. The selection of photographers, writers, and performers is tied to the thematic direction, resulting in an eclectic array of contributors. Our strongest issues present a deft mix of original research, writing, and inventive imagery. Several issues are devoted exclusively to a collaboration with a single choreographer. Our latest *2wice* projects move our black box collaborations into the realm of film and digital media.

How to Pass, Kick, Fall, and Run (2007) borrows its title from a 1965 dance by Merce Cunningham. The issue explores the theme of "how-to," ranging from conceptual art to 1950s etiquette. In a series of photographs shot by Jens Umbach, dancer Tom Gold performs amid dance notation, shown as a 1920s constructivist in a proletariat jumpsuit and in a white suit covered in graphics from a 1950s "how to dance" book.

VISUAL AND PERFORMING ARTS

VOL 9 : NO 2

2wice

HOW
TO
PASS
KICK
FALL
AND
RUN

Feet (1997) was our debut issue, establishing our connection to dance while signaling a more idiosyncratic perspective. Art, photography, fashion, dance, and furniture were featured as provocative tangents on the theme. The cover image, shot by James Wojcik, is a Caravaggio-like still life featuring the foot of a famous foot model that I interviewed for the issue.

Interiors (1997) twisted the genre of shelter magazines in a more esoteric direction. The issue includes Timothy Hursley's photographs of legal brothels in Nevada, Andy Warhol's apartment in Paris, rarefied antiques, Duane Michals's photographs of Giorgio Morandi's studio, and Robert Polidori's images of Versaille, which are also featured on the cover.

NIGHT
WATCH

Louis XVI grand bronze clock on wooden base.
Movement by D. F. Dubois, Paris, circa 1785.
From the collection of Steve Brothers, Inc.

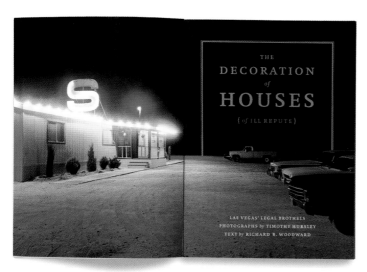

THE
DECORATION
of
HOUSES
{ of ILL REPUTE }

LAS VEGAS' LEGAL BROTHELS
PHOTOGRAPHS by TIMOTHY HURSLEY
TEXT by RICHARD B. WOODWARD

VISUAL \ CULTURE \ DOCUMENT   VOL 1 : NO 2

2wice

INTERIORS

VISUAL \ CULTURE \ DOCUMENT   VOL 2 : NO 2

2wice

magazine of the year 1998
society of publication designers

uniform

todd oldham
annette meyer
nudie
geoffrey beene
stewardesses
richard martin
maids
karen kimmel
doormen
cadets
wonder woman
geisha
superman
mark wigley
bunny
the art guys
muzak

Uniform (1998) contains fantastic material: Arthur Golden on geishas; Laura Jacobs on stewardesses; images of cadets, superheroes, and clothes made of food packaging by artist Annette Meyer. With permission from the Museum of the Fashion Institute of Technology we photographed and annotated the components of a Playboy bunny uniform.

As we developed the issue I recalled a story that when Massimo Vignelli and his colleagues came from Italy to establish a design studio in Chicago, they wore white lab coats to signal their credentials as rational modernists in the European mold. I wrote to Vignelli expecting to hear that the story was more legend than truth, but he sent me back a friendly note with a dashing three-quarter profile shot.

bunny

AFTERNOON OF A
FAUN

ALEXANDRE PROIA
Photography by Martin Schoeller

Restaging was a consistent theme in *2wice*, both in re-creating dances for documentation, and in basing new imagery on historic precedents. For *Animal* (2003) we worked with dancer Alexandre Proia and photographer Martin Schoeller to restage *The Afternoon of a Faun* as an homage to the famous 1912 dance performed by Vaslav Nijinsky. For *Picnic* (2003) a group of dancers performed variations on Manet's 1863 *The Luncheon on the Grass*, photographed by Tony Rinaldo.

For an essay on doormen in *Uniform* (1998), I juxtaposed a 1915 photograph of a doorman with a mirrored version we staged at the Mercer Hotel, photographed by Graham MacIndoe. The formality of the historic image is contrasted with the lanky doorman, whose anti-uniform emphasizes his role as décor more than as a provider of an essential service.

INSIDE

Interiors (1997) turns
clothing by Comme
des Garçons and
Geoffrey Beene inside
out, photographed by
Jay Zukerkorn.

PICNIC

Picnic (2003) explores rustic and rarefied social rituals of dining *en plein air*. I commissioned a Hong Kong tailor to create a gingham suit for choreographer Mark Morris. His friendly picnic persona is featured on a life-size poster celebrating awards and exhibitions for *2wice*, but his vengeful, knife-wielding picnic warrior is hidden under the flaps of the cover. Sarah Blodgett's close-up photographs of insects are a reminder of the natural world.

VISUAL AND PERFORMING ARTS

VOL 7 : NO 1

2wice

animal

Animal (2003) is literal—presenting photographs of real, fake, and skeletal animals, as well as metaphorical—representing choreography that contrasts propriety and restraint against animalistic and savage tendencies. The issue includes photographs by Christian Witkin of a 1976 piece called *Cloven Kingdom* by the Paul Taylor Dance Company and, on the cover, Ashley Leite from Stephen Petronio Company.

School in Lynchburg, he headed the hop committee.) Taylor is a habitual observer of animal behavior. He is a dog lover. He is a butterfly collector. Insects fascinate him. (Jitter! Bug!)

People, too, he knows well, although we perhaps appeal to him less, given as we are to various deceptions unknown in the lower kingdoms. (Animals may perform, but they don't

Green World (2007) is an ambitious restaging of Merce Cunningham's 1994 dance *Ocean* in the gardens of Vizcaya, a historic estate in Miami. The issue unfolds slowly, meandering through the gardens at dawn, glimpsing statuary amid the lush vegetation. Cunningham carefully arranged every movement during our daylong shoot. In Katherine Wolkoff's photographs, the dancers emerge like peacocks with an eruption of iridescent blue within the dense green of Vizcaya. Once the dance is completed, the pages capture details of the vegetation, the surface of the water, and the creatures that inhabit the garden.

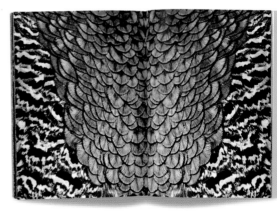

HOW TO BE A GURU

THE ONLY WAY TO DO IT IS TO DO IT.   MERCE CUNNINGHAM

How to be a Guru (2007) captures
practice sessions at the Merce
Cunningham studio. Photographed
by Katherine Wolkoff, the images
are arranged as a panorama across
sixteen pages, using the windows to
define scale and rhythm. In the
same issue, images from a rehearsal
at Mark Morris's studio are knit
together to describe a full rotation
through the studio. The bars of the
Mozart score of the dance provide a
graphic baseline to the layout.

Look at these pictures of the Merce Cunningham Dance Company in their beautiful light-filled studio in the Westbeth Building in New York, and imagine a figure just out of sight.

26

27

It seems to take place in spring, in abundant happiness, and is chock-full of brilliant devices for entrances and exits.

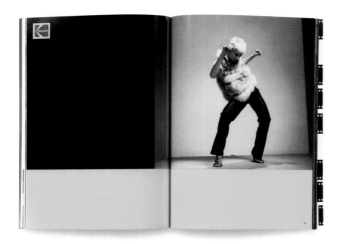

VISUAL AND PERFORMING ARTS   VOL 5 : NO 1

2wice

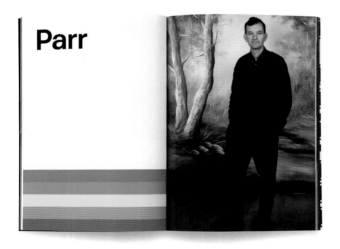

Parr

Photography figures prominently in the thematic evolution of *2wice*. *Camera* (2001) looks at the role of the apparatus, including different types of cameras, lenses, and brands of film. *Everybody Dance Now* (2009) is devoted to Martin Parr's photographs of social dancing, taken over the course of thirty years.

**Blackpool
England
2007**

EVERY
BODY

PHOTOGRAPHS BY MARTIN PARR

DANCE
NOW

editions/wwe

**Durban
South Africa
2005**

**Dubai
UAE
2007**

**Paris
France
2005**

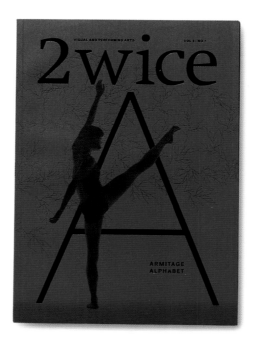

Armitage Alphabet (2006) is a collaboration with choreographer Karole Armitage. The issue creates a narrative arc through the transformation of the sets, color, and graphic reproduction techniques. The ensemble of dancers were placed in a landscape we created with a system of interconnecting branches designed by Ronan and Erwan Bouroullec. The images, photographed by Patrick Giardino, were manipulated through alternations of color and resolution.

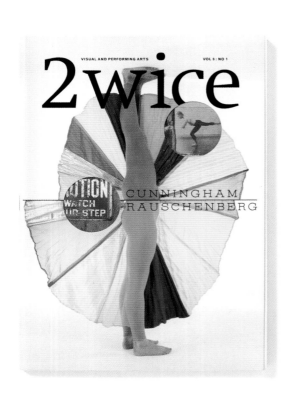

Cunningham/Rauschenberg
(2006) features costumes created
by Robert Rauschenberg for
dances choreographed by Merce
Cunningham. Many of these
groundbreaking works—produced
from the 1950s until 2007—were
never properly documented.
We restaged the dances with
Cunningham directing every movement on the set for photographer
Joachim Ladefoged.

The images wrap over the edges
of the Japanese binding, suggesting
a continuous performance space.
Titles of the dances punctuate the
space, rendered in metallic foil
stamped letters, set in a custom
typeface called 2wice Egyptienne
by Chester Jenkins.

At a party to celebrate the launch
of the issue there was a memor-
able moment when I was having a
conversation with Cunningham,
Rauschenberg, and Jasper Johns,
three icons of modernism gathered
around *2wice*.

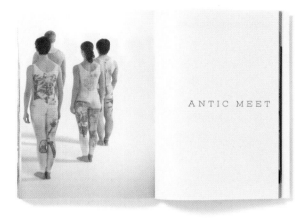

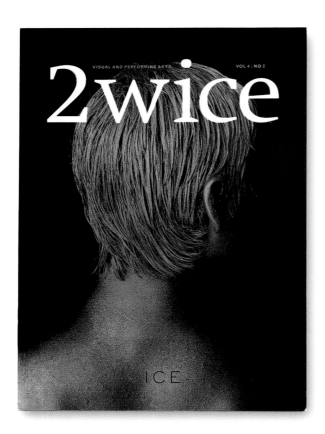

Ice (2000) includes images of icebergs and arctic exploration alongside performers rendered in icy silver and blue tones. New York City Ballet soloist Tom Gold, painted in head-to-toe silver, was transformed into art deco statuary in photographs by Andrew Eccles. The irridescent cover is printed on a spectral paper that creates an ambiguous, holographic depth.

False Start (2008) focuses on a single piece of choreography, Jonah Bokaer's *False Start.* Conceived as a ninety-six-page flipbook, the issue lets the reader reanimate the dance by flipping backwards and forwards, or by viewing it as a series of still frames. Left-hand pages feature a numerical display, traced in stencils, that recall Bokaer's inspiration, a painting by Jasper Johns titled *False Start*.

editions2wice

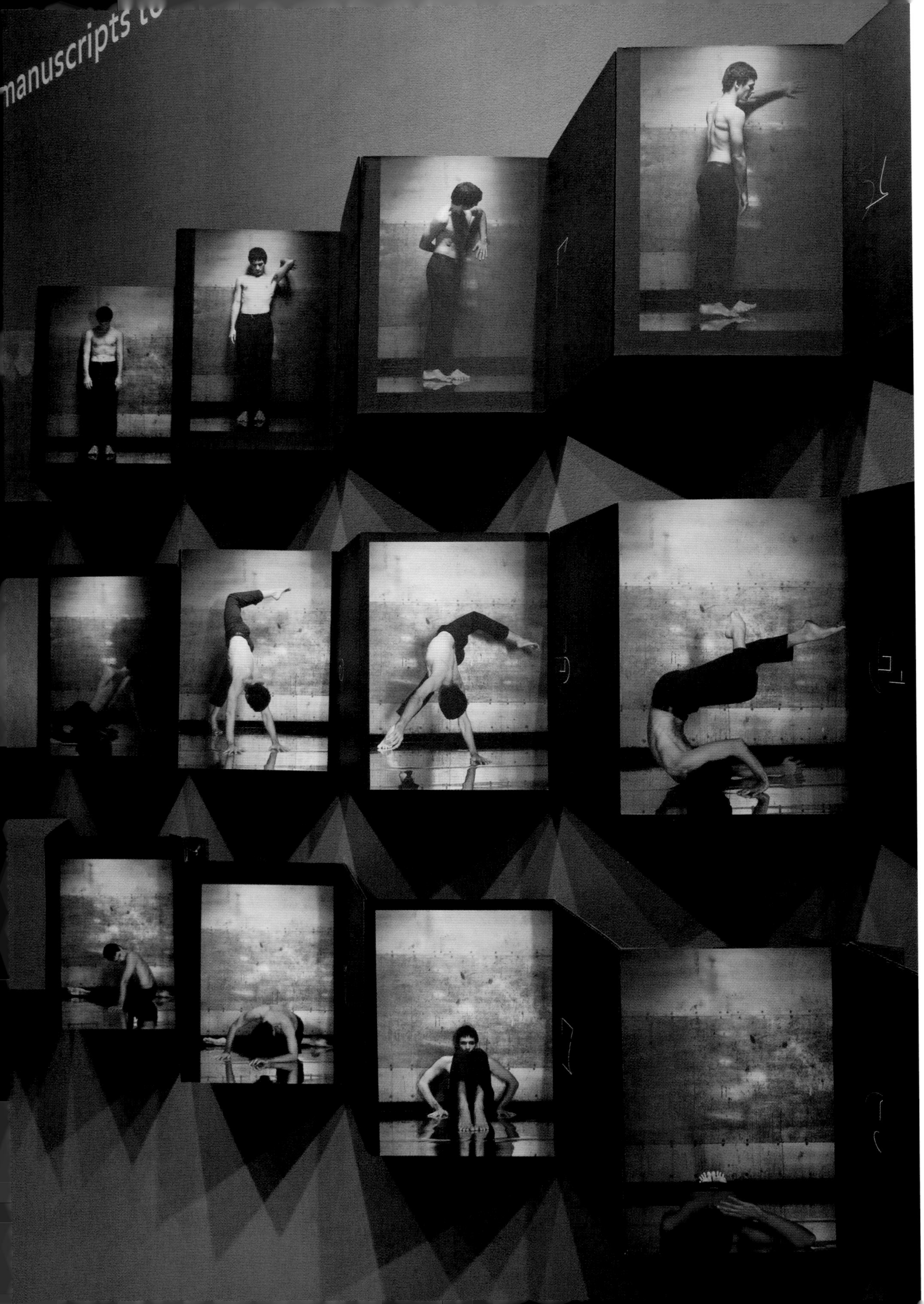
manuscripts to

you have to love dancing to stick to it. it gives you nothing back, no manuscripts to store away, no paintings to show on walls and maybe hang in museums, no poems to be printed and sold, nothing but that single fleeting moment when you feel alive. it is not for unsteady souls. MERCE CUNNINGHAM

Everybody Dance Now (2009) was a survey exhibition of *Dance Ink* and *2wice* at the AIGA National Design Center in New York. Pages and covers from the magazines were displayed on accordion-folded structures made of galvanized metal. A metal shop in Baltimore that manufactures air-conditioning ducts fabricated the elements—an inexpensive display system that, when paired with a disco ball, created an industrial glamour. We used History—a varied and ornamental font by Peter Bil'ak—for the window graphics, posters, and invitations.

Fifth Wall (2012) is an app that conceives the digital tablet as a new performance space. My concept for *Fifth Wall* was to construct a box based on the exact proportions of an iPad, collaborating with choreographer Jonah Bokaer to create a dance that responds to the slippery orientation and gravitational dynamics of the device. Bokaer's performance took place within a shallow box that confounds a fixed sense of gravity, highlighting the way the user's movement and interactions constantly impact the representation of the dance. The accelerometer—the mechanism that reorients the screen by shifting between landscape or portrait view in response to the user's orientation—provided a foil to the movement of the dancer.

To the "natural" disorientation of the medium, we added several in-camera pivots from landscape to portrait, as well as full rotations of the box itself (pushed by me), revealing the constructed nature of the box. The user can move and rescale individual boxes as they display full motion video, and also select frame-within-frame views. The footage was shot by Ben Nicholas and the app was programmed by Eddie Opara and his team at Pentagram. The original score is by So Percussion.

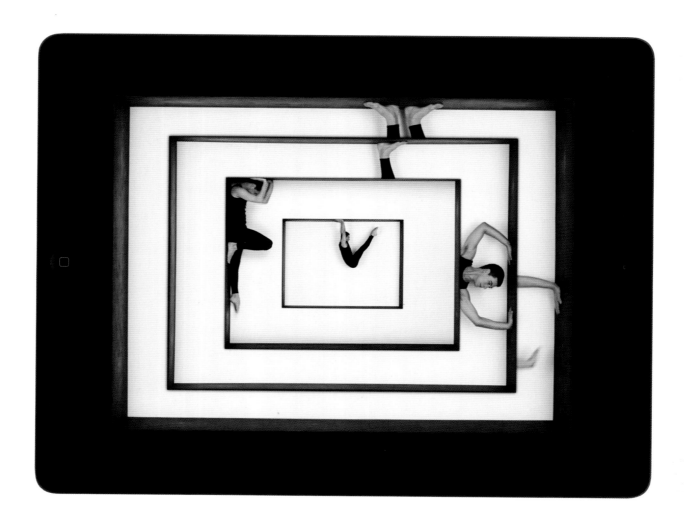

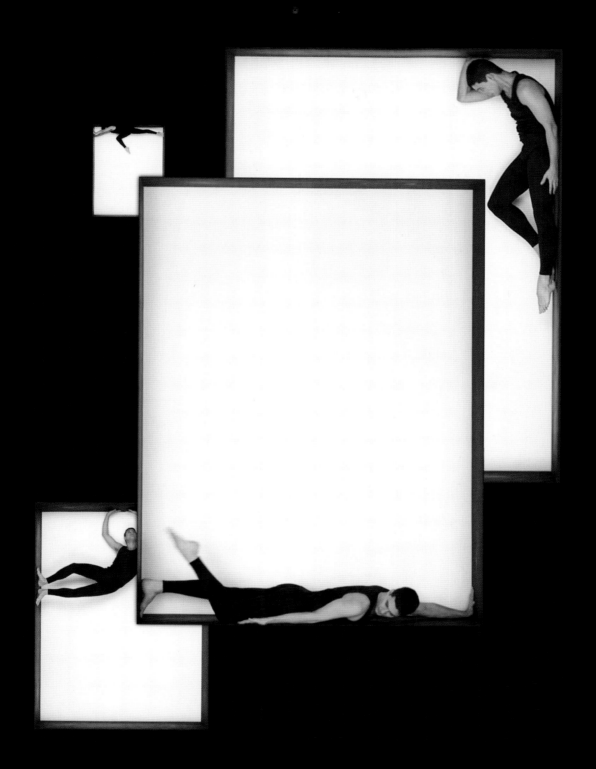

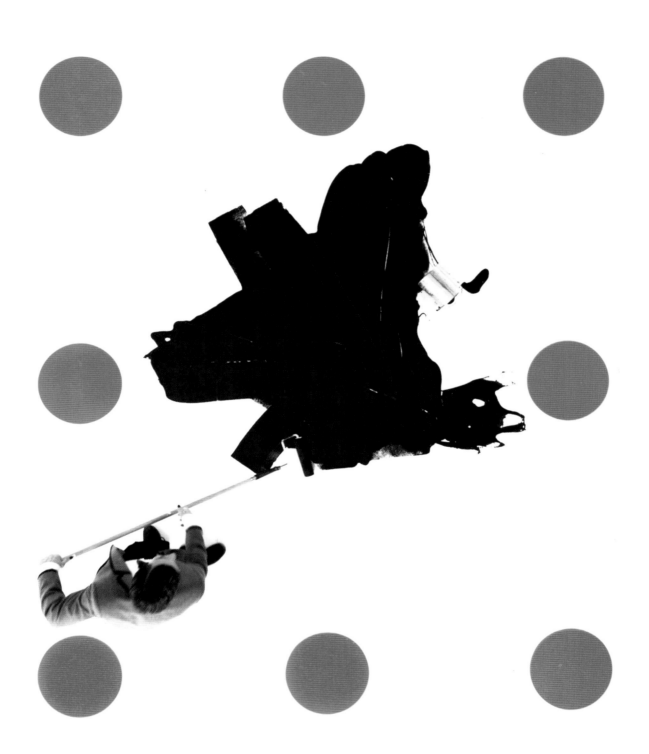

Dot Dot Dot (2013) creates a playful parallel between the touch-screen interface of the digital tablet and the performance stage. The project is a collaboration with choreographer and dancer Tom Gold. On a specially constructed stage, designed to the proportions of the iPad, a series of nine "buttons" create a touch-sensitive landscape. Based on the user's finger movements, *Dot Dot Dot* allows the user to shift between different actions and views. The footage was shot by Ben Nicholas, and violinist Charles Yang created the score. At left, the performer kicks over a can of black paint and improvises a duet with his paint roller.

patterns create patterns from patterns

The degradation of avant-garde artistic practices into the kitsch of mass culture is often illustrated by Jackson Pollock's drip paintings, which "inspired" wallpaper, Formica, and other surfaces. The Pollock-to-Formica story has been portrayed as a cautionary tale of how serious fine art becomes banal when pressed into the service of daily life. Designers don't face these anxieties and are, instead, inspired by the opportunity to bring their work into everyday life.

When I was invited to design wallpaper for Knoll, I decided to derive patterns from the raw materials of my work by using typographic forms. While "normal" uses of type involve optimizing scale, spacing, and margins for legibility, creating *patterns* from type meant setting it for purely optical effects. I called the first series of patterns the Grammar Collection, referring to the idea that typography forms a visual grammar, as well as alluding to the literary dimension of type. A second collection called Ink investigated the behavior of ink on paper, reflecting on the status of wallpaper as ink on vertical surfaces.

In designing a series of patterns for Formica I was drawn to the idea of creating something inspired by the medium of print. Because Formica begins life as a sheet of printed paper, I developed patterns that refer to offset printing: the transparency of ink, the minute scale of dotscreen, and the different values created through benday dots.

The Ink collection (2011) was generated through drawings that explored the behavior of ink on paper. The patterns were derived from: dots formed by plopping ink from a dropper, branching clusters formed by tilting the surface of the paper and letting ink run, and letterforms that resulted from deliberately "steering" the ink to form them.

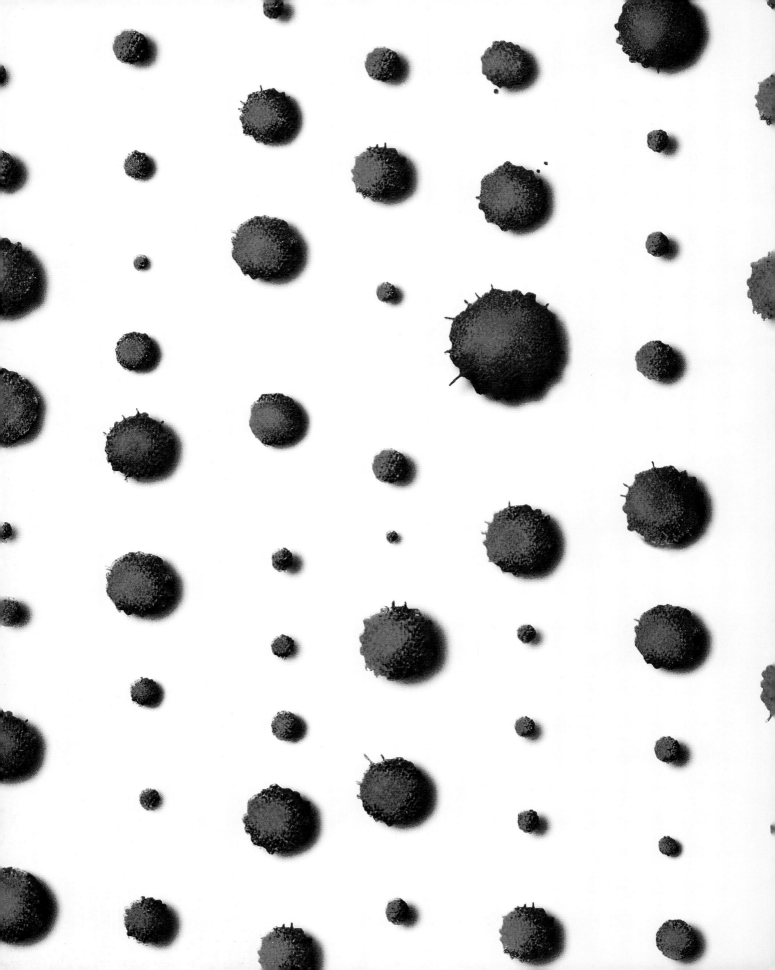

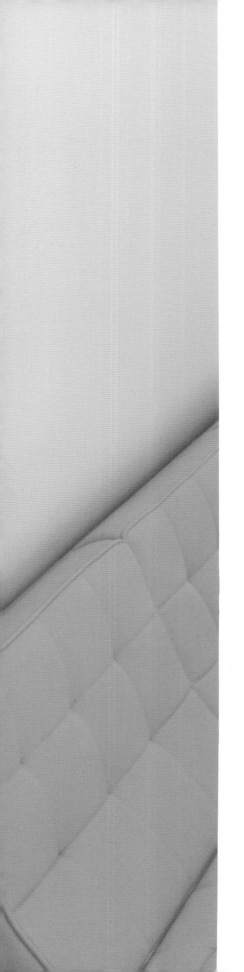

The Grammar collection (2006)
was based on the repetition of
typographic characters to create
a densely woven texture.
The patterns carry the spirit of
the fonts they are based on
but suppress the recognition of
individual marks. The spaces
between characters provide
hints of the forms—brief cracks
in a wall of signs.

The Formica Anniversary Collection (2013) was created for the company's centennial. The pattern Audio was based on the idea of a "digital grain"—a texture that has the scale of wood grain but rendered in a geometric language. Ellipse plays with the transparent characteristics of printing. The implied oval of the Formica logo is super-imposed on itself in a randomized pattern that only repeats every two hundredth sheet.

Dotscreen and Halftone refer to Formica's basis in printing technology. These micropatterns read as nearly solid from a distance, but at close range their patterning animates the surface. The series brings brighter, more complex hues to the Formica palette, acknowledging the prevalence of color in the company's history.

a book is a movie you hold in your hands

Books collapse space and time into volumes that, like an accordion, expand and contract with the action of reading. They are physical objects of a certain size and weight, and they are also a kind of "score" for the reader's experience. Designers affect both aspects, determining a book's appearance—how it feels in a material sense—as well as how a reader navigates its terrain. Throughout history, books have "learned" from other media. In the 1920s, El Lissitzky and László Moholy-Nagy reexamined the book in relation to avant-garde experiments in photography and cinema. These relatively new media reinvigorated the tradition-bound medium of book design. Photography allowed designers to conceptualize the book as having an experiential dimension analogous to film, thereby opening up new ways of thinking about the structure, rhythm, and content of books.

The simple and instinctual act of turning the pages of a book is as elegant an interface as any imaginable. A new lexicon of interaction is evolving in digital media that will steadily influence the physical form and conceptual organization of printed books as well as their status and distribution. But as new media defines new models for authors, designers, and publishers, it simultaneously refines our notion of what is specific to the medium of the printed book. Design in books is especially interesting now because digital media is forcing us to claim, defend, and define their physicality. Inventive uses of materials and techniques can bring a tactile and sensual dimension to books that deepens the reader's experience. Books are a temporal and spatial arena—an immersive space whose wholeness is characterized by cuts and folds and the "thickness" of the user's interactions. Books may aspire to be filmic, but they want to seduce the hand as well as the eye.

The role of the book designer is to deepen the connection between form and content, to make books a vivid and irreplaceable medium for authors, readers, and designers. This is especially important as texts migrate into other media, proliferate into myriad formats and excerpts, and become increasingly "placeless." Just as certain businesses depend upon brick-and-mortar environments to establish their identity and authenticity, certain types of content demand a compelling physical realization. The fundamental pleasure we take in books—their combination of stability and tactility—sets a high bar for the evolution of electronic interfaces. Books remind us of a statement by Charles Eames: "Take your pleasures seriously."

The Cremaster Cycle, 2003

The Cremaster Cycle (2003) documents Matthew Barney's epic five-part film and the drawing, photography, and sculpture he produced as part of that oeuvre. Curated by Nancy Spector, the exhibition occupied most of the Guggenheim Museum. The book functioned as a catalog to the exhibition and a guide to the sensibilities and themes of the project. The greatest challenge was how to organize so much material. During our meetings in Barney's studio a large wall was covered with the storyboard for *Cremaster Five*, then in development. Location shots, drawings on notecards, images of sculptures in progress, and photographs torn from magazines were pinned into a sequence that roughly tracked the narrative arc of the film. We seized on the storyboard's mix of sources as a way to structure the book, avoiding a more straightforward organization by medium.

With its large format, self-consciously elegant typography (Didot), and wide margins, the book design references the refined and analytical character of an encyclopedia. Exaggerated thumb tabs mark the beginning of each film in *The Cremaster Cycle*. Through precision, detail, and depth, the book parallels the obsessive nature of Barney's practice. It uses the language of rational exposition to present work whose coordinates are sexual, psychological, and irrational.

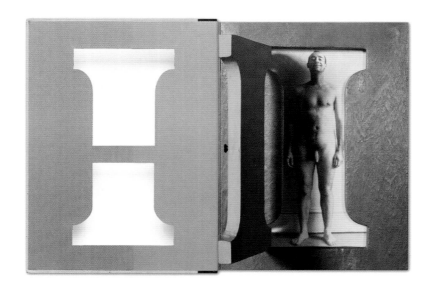

Robert Morris: The Mind/Body Problem (1994) surveys the artist's work on the occasion of a retrospective at the Guggenheim Museum. Robert Morris's own use of slab serif fonts within his objects and paintings established the books typographic sensibility. The cover is based on a 1962 piece titled *I-Box*—a small box featuring an I-shaped door opens to reveal a photograph of Morris, naked and cheerful. The raw board binding features a die-cut letter *I*, with a bar that both shelters and censors Morris. As the reader opens the book the door is shown on the left in its opened state, creating a parallel experience between the sculpture and the book.

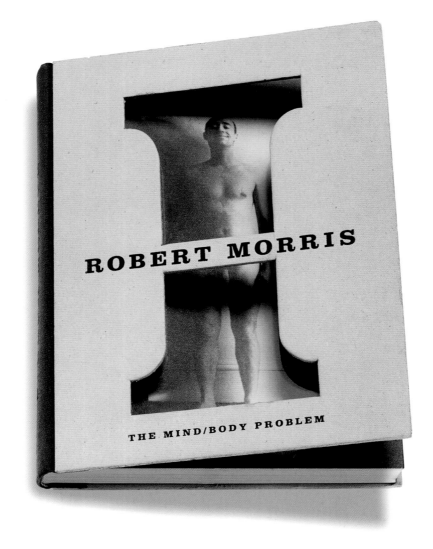

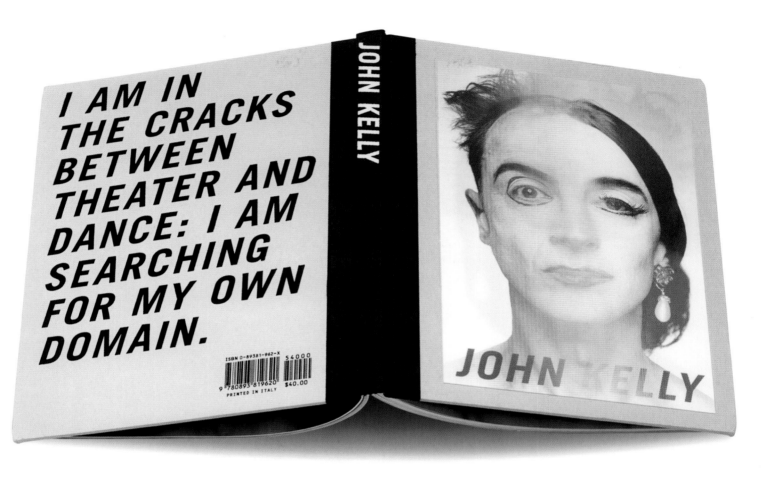

Diary of a Somnambulist

If this were the 1920s, I'd be in Hollywood or Europe, acting in movies. I love silent movies. It's like choreography. The movement is the language—dramatic, beautiful and poetic.

The idea for *Diary of a Somnambulist* came from the 1919 German Expressionist film, *The Cabinet of Dr. Caligari*. In the film, Cesare is a somnambulist manipulated by the mysterious Dr. Caligari into committing a series of murders. The hallmark of this silent classic was its exclusive use of black-and-white sets constructed and hand painted in an extremely stylized manner.

The notion of an alluring creature controlled by an outside force amidst this fantastic monochromatic dreamscape became my point of departure. We restricted the design pallet of the performance (costume, makeup, film and setting) to black and white. Dr. Caligari was present metaphorically, by way of a small cut out figure spinning slowly but incessantly on a hidden turntable. For dramatic tension, I instead paired Cesare with another sleepwalker from the history of art—Lady MacBeth, played by the brilliant Marleen Menard, accompanied by Verdi's music rather than Shakespeare's verse.

Marleen, whom I met at the Pyramid Club, was an ex-dancer like me and has been an inspirational performing partner and muse for me. She has a beautiful deep voice and incredible presence. I was always getting her to do things she may have resisted at first. With Lady MacBeth, I thought of walking, she walks the halls at night, walking, walking, racked with guilt, wringing her hands. Huck constructed this treadmill, and Marleen was to

John Kelly (2001) captures New York's Lower East Side cabaret scene of the early 1980s as it documents the artist's unique form of visual theater. The book reveals his talents as a writer, vocalist, actor, and costume and set designer. We developed the book together, tracing his intensively researched productions through sketchbooks, photographs, and journals. His fluid portrayal of male and female characters led us to use a lenticular cover, juxtaposing a character based on the paintings of Egon Schiele and "Dagmar Onassis," the fictional illegitimate love child of Maria Callas and Aristotle Onassis. Flashes of fluorescent red ink are a nod to the eighties East Village scene that provided the context in which we both came of age.

The Furniture of Charles and Ray Eames (2007) was designed for Vitra, the Swiss company that has manufactured Eames designs for the European market since the 1950s. The book shows the larger context of the Eameses' practice and the way in which the designers pioneered different constructive techniques in furniture. The mixture of historic and contemporary images required a specific strategy for staging their relationship. I developed a kind of "shelf" that runs through the book: archival images are seen as a back-drop to the contemporary productions. The horizontal flow of content is divided into sections by a yellow "speed bump" that announces a new zone of content. The ovoid "vitra eames" logo was a collaboration with Tibor Kalman, who first introduced me to Rolf Fehlbaum, the visionary CEO of Vitra.

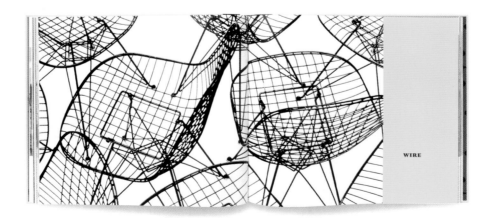

charles & ray

la chaise

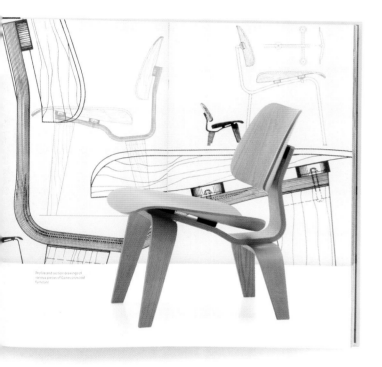

Profile and section drawings of various pieces of Eames plywood furniture

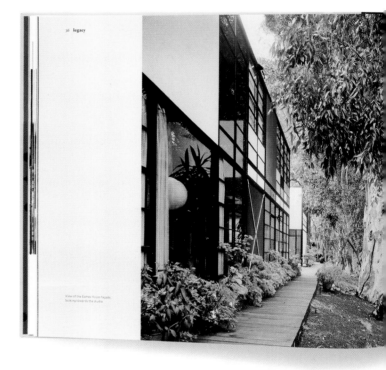

36 legacy

View of the Eames House façade, looking towards the studio

vitra.
eames

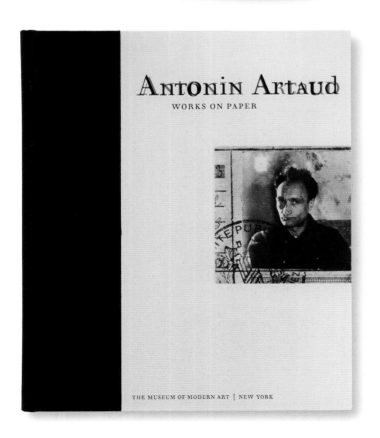

ANTONIN ARTAUD
WORKS ON PAPER

THE MUSEUM OF MODERN ART | NEW YORK

"Le visage humain…"
ANTONIN ARTAUD : JUNE 1947

The human face
is an empty force, a
field of death.
The old revolutionary
demand for a form
that has never corres-
ponded to its body, that started
off as something other
than the body.
Thus is it absurd
to denounce the academicism
of a painter
who currently
persists in reproducing
the features of the human face
such as they are; for such
as they are they have not
yet found the form that they
promise and designate;
and do better than outlining
pounding away at it
from morning to night,
and in the midst of ten thousand dreams,
as in the crucible of a passional
palpitation never wearied.
Which means
that the human visage
hasn't yet found its face
and that it behooves the painter
to find it in its place.
Which means however
that the human visage
such as it is still looks
for itself with two eyes a
nose a mouth
and the two auricular
cavities
which answer the holes
of the orbits as
the four openings

Le visage humain
est une force vide, un
champ de mort.
La vieille revendication
révolutionnaire d'une forme
qui n'a jamais corres
pondu à son corps, qui partait
pour être autre chose
que le corps.
C'est ainsi qu'il est absurde
de reprocher d'être académique
à un peintre
qui à l'heure qu'il est
s'obstine encore à reproduire
les traits du visage humain
tels qu'ils sont; car tels
qu'ils sont ils n'ont pas
encore trouvé la forme qu'ils
indiquent et désignent;
et font plus que d'esquisser
mais du matin au soir,
et au milieu de dix mille rêves,
pilonnent comme dans le
creuset d'une palpitation
passionnelle jamais lassée.
Ce qui veut dire
que le visage humain
n'a pas encore trouvé sa face
et que c'est au peintre
à la lui donner.
Mais ce qui veut dire
que la face humaine
telle qu'elle est se cherche
encore avec deux yeux un
nez une bouche
et les deux cavités
auriculaires
qui répondent aux trous
des orbites comme
les quatre ouvertures

50 Dessins pour assassiner la magie

"50 Drawings to Assassinate Magic"

It's not a question here of
drawings
in the proper sense of the term,
of somehow incorporating
reality by drawing.
They are not an attempt
to renew
the art
in which I never believed
of drawing
no
but to understand them
you have first to situate them.
These are 50 drawings
culled from various books
of notes
literary
poetic
psychological,
psychological
magical
especially magical
magical first
and foremost,
They are thus interwoven
into pages,
laid down on pages
where the writing
takes up the foreground of
vision,
writing,
the feverish note,
effervescent,
on fire
the blasphemy
the curse.

Il ne s'agit pas ici des
dessins
au propre sens du terme,
d'une incorporation quelconque
de la réalité par le dessin.
Ils ne sont pas une tentative
pour renouveler
l'art
auquel je n'ai jamais cru
du dessin
non
mais pour les comprendre
il faut les situer d'abord
Ce sont 50 dessins
pris à des cahiers
de notes
littéraires
poétiques
psychologiques,
psychologiques
magiques
magiques surtout
magiques d'abord
et par dessus tout.
Ils sont donc entremêlés
à des pages,
couchés sur des pages
où l'écriture
tient le 1er plan de
la vision,
l'écriture,
la note fiévreuse,
effervescente,
ardente
le blasphème
l'imprécation.

From curse to
curse
these pages
progress
and like new
sensitive
bodies
these drawings
are there
to provide commentary,
ventilation
and elucidation
These are not drawings
they figure nothing,
disfigure nothing,
are not there to
construct
edify
establish
a world
be it abstract
These are notes,
words,
shanks,
and being on fire
corrosive
incisive
spurted forth
from who-knows what
vortex of
sub maxillary,
sub spatular
vitriol,
they are there as if
nailed in place
fated not to
make another move.
Mere shanks
but ready to carry out
their apocalypse
for they have spoken
too much of it to be born
and spoken too much in birth
not to be reborn
and
take on body
at last   authentically.

D'imprécation en
imprécation
ces pages
avancent
et comme des corps de
sensibilité
nouveaux
ces dessins
sont là
qui les commentent,
les aèrent
et les éclairent
Ce ne sont pas des dessins
ils ne figurent rien,
ne défigurent rien,
ne sont pas là pour
construire
édifier
instituer
un monde
même abstrait
Ce sont des notes,
des mots,
des trumeaux,
car ardents,
corrosifs
incisifs
jaillis
de je ne sais quel
tourbillon
de vitriol
sous maxillaire,
sous spatulaire,
ils sont là comme
cloués
et destinés à ne
plus bouger.
Trumeaux donc
mais qui feront
leur apocalypse
car ils en ont trop
dit pour naître
et trop dit en naissant
pour ne pas renaître
et
prendre corps
alors   authentiquement.

---

of the burial chamber of the
impending death.
For the human face,
in fact, wears
a perpetual death of sorts
on its face
which it is incumbent on the painter precisely
to save it from
by restoring
its own features.
For thousands and thousands of years indeed,
the human face has talked
and breathed
and one is under the impression still
that it has not begun to
say what it is and what it knows.
Not a single painter in
the history of art, from Holbein
to Ingres, whom I know of
has succeeded in making it talk,
this face of man. Holbein's portraits
or those of Ingres are but
thick walls that explain
nothing of the ancient mortal architecture
that buttresses the
arches of eyelids
or tails into
the cylindrical tunnel
of the two mural
cavities of the ears.
Van Gogh only
could make of the human
head a portrait
which was the
bursting flare of a
throbbing,
exploded heart.
His own.
Van Gogh's head with
a felt hat
renders null and void
all the attempts at abstract
painting which can be
made after him, until the
end of all eternities.
For this face of a butcher
greedy, projected as though
fired from a cannon, upon

du caveau de la
prochaine mort.
Le visage humain
porte en effet une espèce
de mort perpétuelle
sur son visage
dont c'est au peintre justement
à le sauver
en lui rendant
ses propres traits.
Depuis mille et mille ans en effet
que le visage humain parle
et respire
on a encore comme l'impression
qu'il n'a pas encore commencé à
dire ce qu'il est et ce qu'il sait
et je ne connais pas un peintre dans
l'histoire de l'art, d'Holbein
à Ingres qui, ce visage
d'homme, soit parvenu à
le faire parler. Les portraits
d'Holbein ou d'Ingres sont des
murs épais, qui n'expliquent
rien de l'antique architecture mortelle
qui s'arc-boute sous les
arcs de voûte des paupières
ou s'encastre
dans le tunnel cylindrique
des deux cavités
murales des oreilles.
Le seul van Gogh
a su tirer d'une tête
humaine un portrait
qui soit la
fusée explosive du
battement d'un coeur
éclaté.
Le sien.
La tête de van Gogh au
chapeau mou rend nulles
et non avenues
toutes les tentatives de peintures
abstraites qui pourront être
faites depuis lui, jusqu'à la
fin des éternités.
Car ce visage de boucher
avide, projeté comme
en coup de canon à la surface

Antonin Artaud: Works on Paper
(1996) focuses on a series of
manuscripts produced by the author.
Suffering from illness and addiction,
Artaud spent his later years in
psychiatric institutions where he
was subjected to electroshock
treatments. During this period
he made a series of works on paper
that incorporate words, vengeful
diatribes, and poetic verse written
with idiosyncratic spacing. The
drawings were typically executed
on both sides of the paper, with
cigarette holes burned through their
surfaces. Reproducing the drawings with their two sides facing one
another creates a beautiful
Rorschach-like effect. A similar
symmetry occurs with the mirroring
of the translations, heightened
by the idiosyncratic spacing of the
original texts.

Schiaparelli and Prada: Impossible Conversations (2012) was produced in conjunction with an exhibition at the Metropolitan Museum of Art Costume Institute. Curator Andrew Bolton staged a dialogue between the two fashion designers, finding striking similarities in the work of Miuccia Prada and pioneer Elsa Schiaparelli. A book-within-a-book structure, with small leaves bound into the larger volume, allowed us to insert passages of the fictional conversation throughout the book. The juxtaposition of historic and contemporary imagery creates a contrapuntal rhythm to the pages. The smaller book pages feature text, photographic details, and reference images. The cover follows the same logic: a detail of a Prada skirt—the surrealist lips are a direct reference to Schiaparelli—is printed on a cloth binding; attached to the surface with its own gray cloth spine is an historic image of Schiaparelli's famous shoe hat.

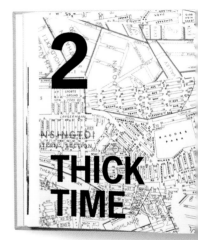

William Kentridge: Five Themes
(2009) was produced for a retrospective of the artist's films, drawings, and sculpture. Telescoping across the page, individual frames convey the nature of Kentridge's approach: each frame is a discrete drawing in itself but also part of a sequence that builds into a filmic whole. Smaller frames emphasize growth and progression over time by gradually stepping up in size until they fill the entire space of the page. The compositional strategy has a gravitational pull toward the bottom of the page, creating a ragged skyline.

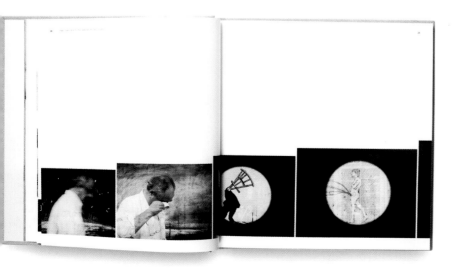

Scanning: The Aberrant Architectures of Diller + Scofidio (2003), a catalog for a retrospective at the Whitney Museum of American Art, features the architects' designs for sets and installations, objects, furniture, and buildings. Sly and subversive, the work in the show dealt with the social and psychological aspects of architecture, technology, surveillance, and global media. The book reflects their fondness for complexity: images wrap around the outer folds of the Japanese binding; perforations at the edge of each page invite readers to tear the book open, revealing images printed on the undersides of pages; elliptical cuts create openings that reveal strange scenes played out in hotel rooms and offices cubicles. The cover features an eight-stage lenticular photograph that animates the hydraulics of a "syringe cocktail."

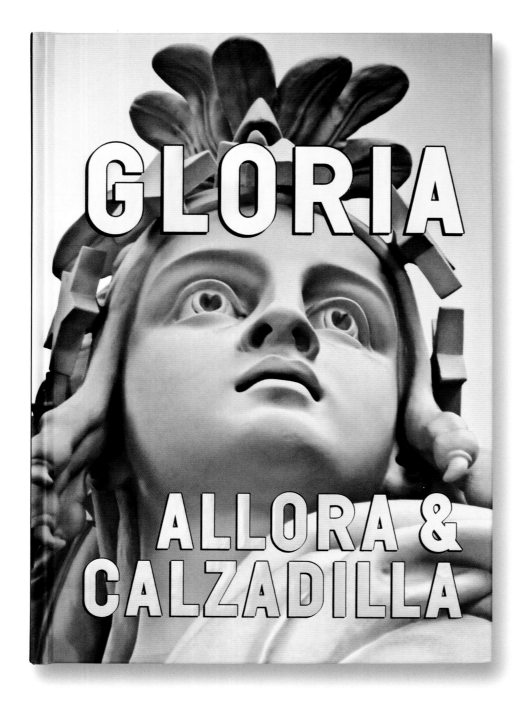

GLORIA

ALLORA & CALZADILLA

Gloria (2011) was produced for an exhibition of the artists Allora & Calzadilla's work in the U.S. Pavilion at the Venice Biennale, a series of sculptural installations that reflected on themes of American identity and power on the international stage. The cover image, a detail of the Statue of Freedom that stands atop the U.S. Capitol building, captures the theatrical and propagandistic pitch of the installations. The exhibition was a surrealist juxtaposition of militarism, patriotism, and competitive sports: a large pipe organ dispensed cash (and also music) through an ATM; an Olympic gymnast performed an acrobatic routine on a replica of business class American Airlines seats; and a treadmill was affixed to the treads of a large military tank in the pavilion's garden.

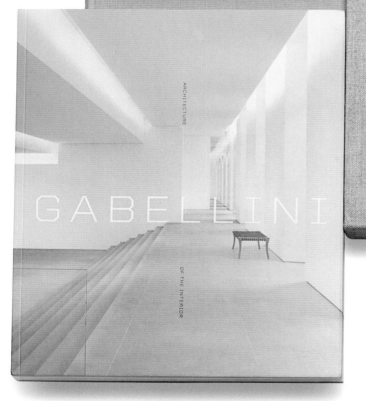

Barney/Beuys: All in the Present
Must be Transformed (2007) uses
typography to mirror the dialogue
between the artists' work. The large
format of *Ansel Adams at 100*
(2003) conveys authority through its
scale and materials. *Gabellini:
Architecture of the Interior* (2008)
uses Wim Crouwel's font Gridnik
to convey the elegant minimalism
of Michael Gabellini's work.

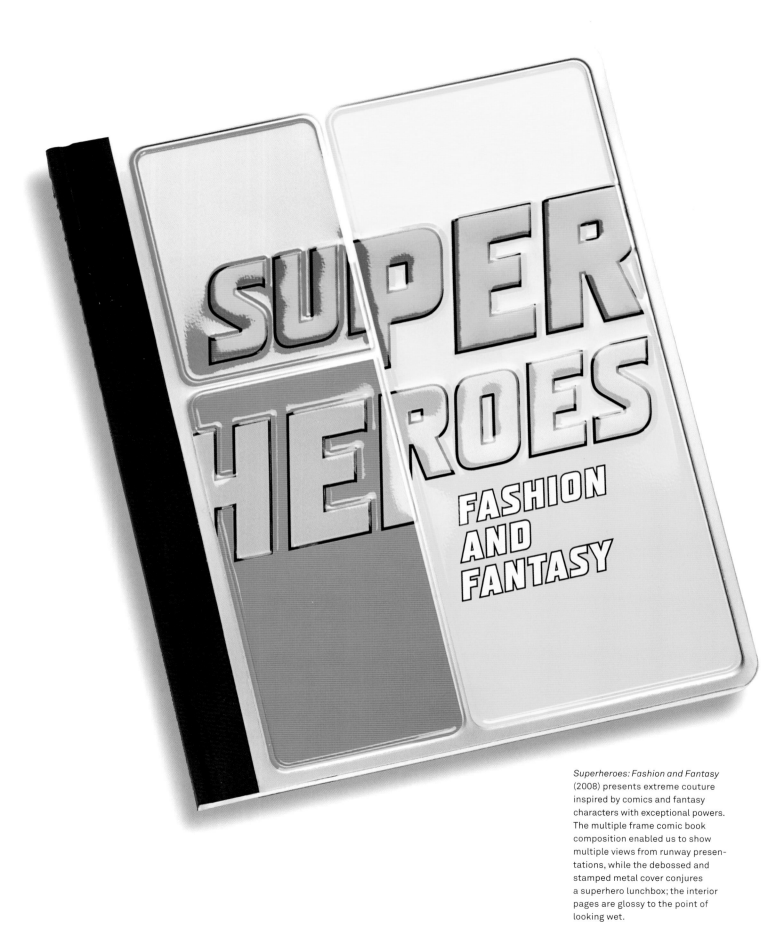

Superheroes: Fashion and Fantasy (2008) presents extreme couture inspired by comics and fantasy characters with exceptional powers. The multiple frame comic book composition enabled us to show multiple views from runway presentations, while the debossed and stamped metal cover conjures a superhero lunchbox; the interior pages are glossy to the point of looking wet.

an exhibition is a room with a plot

Exhibition design creates a physical and interpretive context for objects and images. Unlike the pages of a book, an exhibition presents things in real space and time, delivering a visceral experience that cannot be communicated through reproduction. The environmental dimension of exhibitions connects them to architecture, interior design, and stage design, but their basis in storytelling and interpretation brings them back to editorial design. Exhibition design is a choreography of objects, images, texts, and people: the design shapes how things look and helps audiences construct meaning. Exhibitions simultaneously "stage the object" and "stage the observer." In making decisions about how an object is displayed or a story is told, designers and curators position not only the objects but also the viewers, anticipating their needs and provoking their interest. Exhibition design constructs a stage for both the objects and observers.

The roots of exhibition design are in the fundamentally modern activity of collecting and displaying objects, from the scientific presentation of specimens to the arrangement of goods for sale. From early cabinets of curiosity to the modern museum, techniques for presenting objects and images—frames, pedestals, vitrines, and dioramas—have developed into a repertoire of display strategies. In the 1920s modernist designers and artists reinvigorated (perhaps invented) exhibition design by shifting the emphasis from object to observer. Pioneering exhibition designers such as Frederick Kiesler, Herbert Bayer, El Lissitzky, and Lilly Reich delineated the viewer as a social and dynamic agent of perception. Whereas traditional exhibitions conceived a passive and disembodied viewer, avant-garde designers imagined a dynamic observer, an agent whose perceptions are shaped by his or her position in space and time.

In contemporary exhibition design, conventional museological techniques and radical display strategies coexist. The modernist attention to observers now demands a wider frame of reference—one concerned with the total experience of the viewer/reader—and a broader context of interpretation. New strategies can engage visitors and dramatize their encounter with original artifacts, creating a strong context for ideas when the artifacts themselves fail to tell a complete story.

Exhibition design represents an arsenal of strategies to gain attention in a culture suffused by competing modes of entertainment. The promise of an exhibition is that a face-to-face encounter—with a painting, an object, a physical site—will provide things that cannot be captured in photography, film, or any kind of reproduction; an apprehension of something with the full sensory, bodily impact of direct experience.

Our design for an exhibition about a famous nineteenth-century cemetery creates an environmental tableau from historic maps. Visitors navigate the exhibition encountering objects and stories that are positioned according to their location within the landscape.

A Beautiful Way to Go: New York's Green-Wood Cemetery (2013) presented the history of an urban cemetery that was one of the most important public green spaces in nineteenth-century America. Predating both Central Park and Prospect Park, Green-Wood ultimately influenced the rise of public parks and green space. Its grounds are a museum of monuments and statuary by leading architects and artists, and include the burial places of figures central to the social, political, and cultural life of New York City. The exhibition design gathers artifacts within a range of lantern-like vitrines, conjuring an impression of the cemetery at twilight. A series of maps that document the distinctive, twisting paths and roads of the park are spliced together on the floor, creating a miniaturized landscape. Significant burial plots, and the artifacts and images associated with them, are arranged according to their position on the map.

John Lennon: His Life and Work (2000) was both a celebration and a memorial, since it was produced on the sixtieth anniversary of his birth and the twentieth anniversary of his death. Curated by Jim Henke at the Rock and Roll Hall of Fame and Museum, the exhibition was done in close collaboration with Yoko Ono. In our first meeting in the Dakota building, she took us into her bedroom and showed us the plastic-wrapped evidence bag that was returned to her after Lennon was killed, and his glasses, which sat on her dresser covered with dried blood from twenty years earlier. She wanted to feature both items in the exhibition to advocate for gun control.

The evidence bag and the glasses were visible through small portholes in a vertical cenotaph marked with the date August 7, 1980. Adjacent to this was a large vitrine with sixty lenses holding snapshots and personal effects from Lennon's life. The sixty holes were also featured on the cover of the book.

In contrast to the predominantly dark and theatrical exhibitions at the Rock and Roll Hall of Fame, the Lennon installation followed the spare white-on-white and Fluxus-inspired sensibility of Yoko Ono's work. Many of the photographs in the book and exhibition featured John and Yoko in white clothing in their all-white apartment, playing their white grand piano.

The main exhibition space presented Lennon's guitars, piano, and artifacts from his career with the Beatles and his later collaborations with Yoko. Visitors ascended a spiral stair to a square, high-ceilinged gallery, where we displayed original manu-

scripts of his lyrics. Eight panels placed around the gallery featured enlarged lyrics; in a random sequence the sound of each song emerged from the graphic, using the membrane of the panel as a speaker.

A circular light fixture illuminated the space, highlighting a sequence of large numbers high on each wall: 40 for the year he was born, 60 for what would have been his sixtieth birthday, 80 for the year he died, and 00 for 2000, the year in which the show was held.

Mannahatta (2009) represented a ten-year research project on the ecology and wildlife of Manhattan four hundred years ago, when it was sparsely populated by Lenape Indians. Conducted by landscape ecologist Eric Sanderson, the study used sophisticated sampling and mapping techniques to provide an amazingly detailed picture of the geography, plant life, and wildlife of Manhattan. Markley Boyer used this data to visualize these "lost" landscapes, creating a series of compelling images that became the focal point of the *Mannahatta* book and an exhibition at the Museum of the City of New York. Structures that recall large-format cameras were situated within the gallery, placed in relation to a topographic model of Manhattan, presenting layers of information through digital projection. Different regions and geological features were identified through their historic names but in the style of the New York City subway graphics.

The Rolling Stone Covers Tour (1998) exhibition celebrated thirty years of the magazine's iconic covers. We designed a landscape of sculptural letter fragments derived from the distinctive forms of the magazine's logo. In a series of models we experimented with different ways of rendering the letterforms, using photographic collages to visualize their effect as built forms. It was first exhibited in New York City and traveled to over fifty different locations; the fractured forms of the letters and light boxes were designed for fast breakdown and installation. Because of their sculptural character, the composition of elements could dramatically expand and contract in response to different spaces.

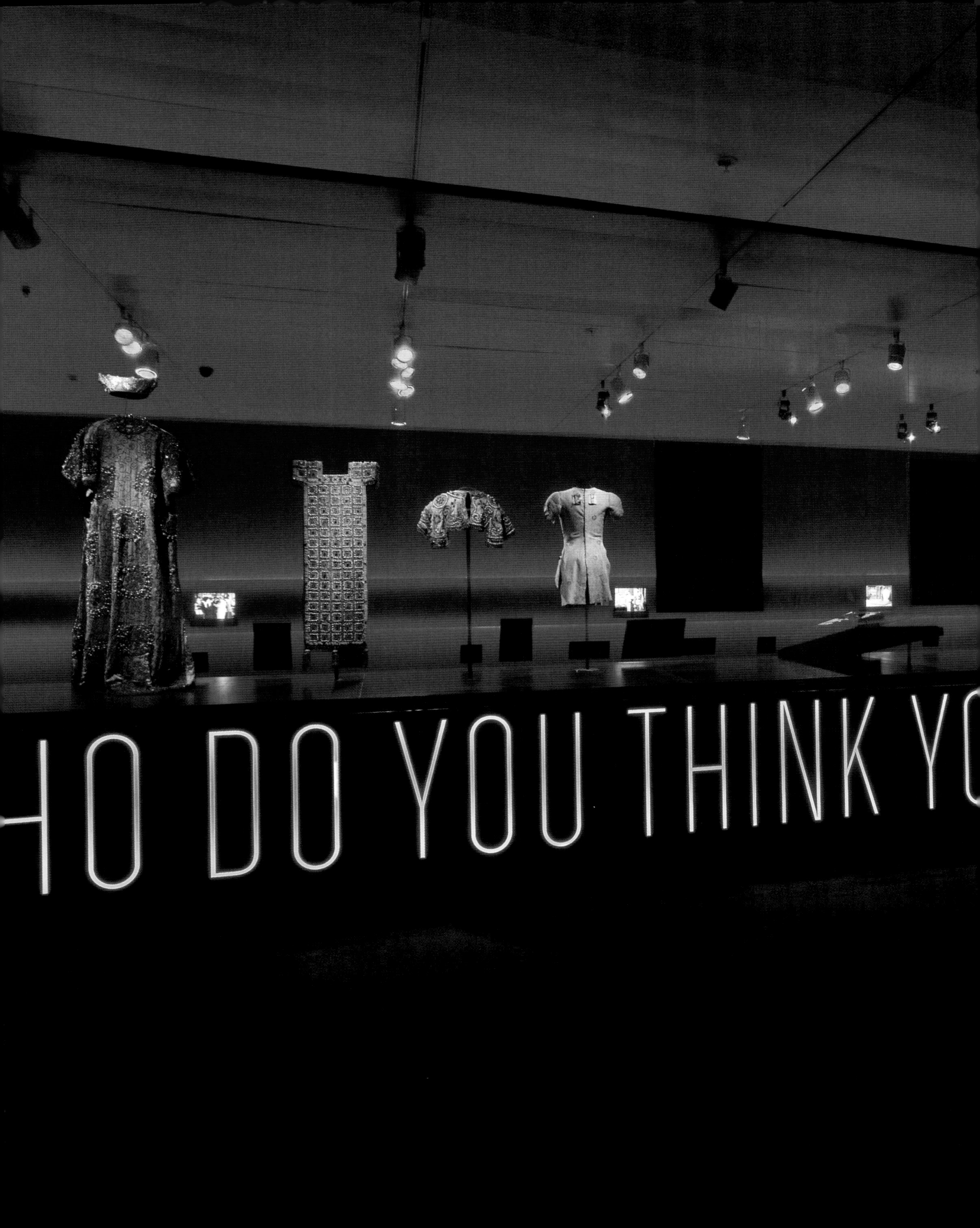
HO DO YOU THINK YO

ARE—SARAH BERNHARDI?

Sarah Bernhardt: The Art of High Drama (2005) was presented at the Jewish Museum New York. Curators Kenneth Silver and Carol Ockman presented the actress as a prodigious talent who defined the modern culture of celebrity. They asked for an exhibition design that was "not your grandmother's Sarah Bernhardt," specifically banning red velvet curtains and potted palms. Emphasizing her role as a legendary stage actress who transitioned into film, the exhibition was dominated by an imposing linear stage that created a surface for costumes and posters, as well as a lower display area for smaller artifacts, photographs, and ephemera. Because of the curator's emphasis on Bernhardt's pivotal role in the emerging medium of film, screens punctuated a glowing blue horizon on the perimeter wall, displaying her career in early cinema.

As viewers approached the gallery, a large projection of Marilyn Monroe greeted them, with a sequence from The Seven Year Itch in which her character comments that the "Dazzledent" toothpaste commercial she is auditioning for would be seen by more people in one night than had ever seen Sarah Bernhardt in the course of her entire career. The back of the stage was visible and emblazoned with the question: "Who do you think you are—Sarah Bernhardt?"—a rhetorical question asked of every melodramatic teenager of a certain period in history.

Cold War Modern: The Domesticated Avant-Garde (2000) examined how elite and popular culture influenced one another in the post–World War II period. Including art, design, and music, the exhibition—curated by Judith Hoos Fox at the Davis Museum—showed that the traffic between "high" and "low" culture moves up and down, but also sideways. We created a "domestic" context by installing a structure in the middle of the gallery that recalled a modernist house of the 1950s. Visitors approached the gallery from above, where concentric rings on the roof of the house—similar to the diagrams that plotted the scope of radiation fallout in the event of nuclear attack—alluded to the pervasive paranoia of the era. The

radiating rings also signalled the role of sound in the exhibition, which featured music that emanated from within the house. Visible from all points within the space, the word MODERN was set in eighteen-foot-tall Monotype Grotesque, overlaid with different definitions of what modern means in the context of art, politics, and literature. On both ends of the gallery we vastly enlarged a collage of furniture shapes that Irving Harper had developed for an exhibition at the Museum of Modern Art. I was struck by how they distilled the powerful dialogue between art and design that characterized the period. We contacted Harper and he graciously granted us permission.

Rock Style (2000) presented the costumes and stage personae of iconic performers such as the Beatles, Madonna, Mick Jagger, David Bowie, and the Talking Heads. For the exhibition, curated by Jim Henke at the Rock and Roll Hall of Fame and Museum, our strategy was to make visitors feel like they were at the edge of the stage. An open frame vocabulary of pipes, ramps, and decks created a spatially dynamic environment. To accommodate the density of artifacts we created a two-level structure so visitors could ascend to a position halfway between levels, creating constantly shifting sight lines. The tilted planes and loud music created a dynamic and immersive experience.

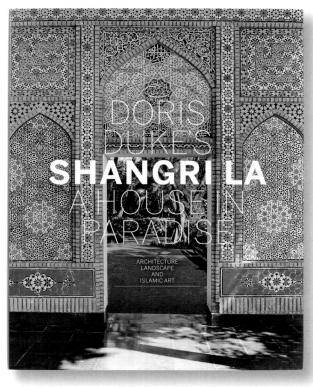

Doris Duke's Shangri La (2013) celebrated the house-as-*Gesamtkunstwerk* in the form of a 1936 villa perched on the ocean in Honolulu. Tobacco-fortune heiress Doris Duke created an idiosyncratic melange of architecture, decorative arts, and gardens based on her travels in the Middle East. The design of the house, by Marion Sims Wyeth, has the simple geometric massing and white surfaces of a modernist structure. However, these forms are a provocative foil to the intricate tilework, inlays, and carved ornamentation that provide the visual thread throughout the estate. This play between modernity and pattern was restaged in the traveling exhibition using white casework and perforated panels—first seen at the Museum of Arts and Design—and in the perforated pages of the book. Photographs by Tim Street-Porter were seen in large-format light boxes that enveloped and transported the viewer to this oceanside retreat.

Mah Jongg: Crack, Bam, Dot (2010) was developed as a traveling exhibition and book documenting the bicultural heritage of the game. Curator Melissa Martens, from the Museum of Jewish Heritage, proposed the concept for the show and together we developed content for the book that explored the intersection of Asian and Jewish cultures in the history of mah jongg. Highlights of the book include: Bruce McCall's image of Chinese elders tutoring ladies in Miami; Maira Kalman's mah jongg murder mystery; and Christoph Niemann's revised mah jongg tiles featuring bagels and dreidels. Our mah jongg pavilion was designed as a modular kit of parts. It took advantage of the height of the museum's high-ceilinged gallery but could be adjusted to lower ceilings in subsequent venues. The proportions of the tiles and their rounded corners provided a language for the display framework, connecting in a lattice structure at the top to form a Jewish star. The typography is adapted from lettering that, like the game, is assembled by arranging tiles.

Valentina (2009) profiled the designer who dominated American and Hollywood fashion for decades and heavily influenced succeeding generations. Curated by Kohle Yohannan and Phyllis Magidson for the Museum of the City of New York, the exhibition was composed of one large gallery, completely black, with a U-shaped runway suspended by aircraft cables. Supporting documents and videos were arrayed on the surface of the deck. The geometry of the tensioned cables was juxtaposed with the designer's name in letters that echoed the diagonal lines of the cabling.

DESIGN
SIGNATURES

Village Works (1999) presented photographs created by women living in mountain villages in Yunnan, China. The project resulted from an experimental initiative funded by the Ford Foundation that teaches illiterate women how to document their daily lives through photography. The goal of the project's creator, Caroline Wang, was to allow women to give voice to their problems through images. By exposing the difficult living conditions for women and children in rural China, these images became a tool for human rights groups to advocate for social change and political support.

The curators, Lucy Flint-Gohlke and Corinne Fryhle, were interested in how the project fused political and aesthetic concerns. The images posed special challenges: the convention of framed photographic prints, particularly in the context of an art museum, would place undue emphasis on their status as works of art. Since the project was rooted in daily life, we adopted the metaphor of the exhibition as

a marketplace at the center of a village. The design of the structures is based on the forms of Chinese characters. We developed the design by translating Chinese phrases such as "photography" and "women" into sculptural constructions. The kitelike construction used welded aluminum and digital images transferred to paper and silk.

The posters for The Couch: Thinking in Repose (2006) feature icons of historic couches by Mies van der Rohe and Charles and Ray Eames, and a turn-of-the-century chaise produced by Thonet specifically for the emerging field of psychoanalysis. Presented as vertical totems, they underscore the difference between repose and the verticality of waking life.

staging psychoanalysis

The design of the exhibition The Couch: Thinking in Repose (2006) was based on the unique circumstances of its site. The Sigmund Freud Museum in Vienna is housed in the apartment that Freud shared with his family for forty-seven years before they emigrated to London in the final years of his life. The museum houses temporary exhibition space and a permanent installation of photographs, furniture, and antiquities that populated Freud's consulting room. What visitors do not see—other than in photographs—is the famous couch, which traveled to London with most of the Freud family possessions in 1938 after the Nazi annexation of Austria. The recurring question from visitors—"But where is the couch?"—inspired this exhibition focused on Freud's theorization of "thinking in repose." Due to government restrictions, it was not possible to borrow the couch from London (it is considered a National Heritage Object) for the exhibition in Vienna, nor could we exhibit the museum's collection of rugs—objects equally redolent of the historical and cultural milieu of psychoanalysis in Vienna.

The exhibition was housed in the apartment above the Freud Museum: the previous tenant had recently vacated it to live in a nursing home. When we first explored the possibility of using this apartment, we discovered a space frozen in time. The apartment had never been modernized and carried the traces of its long history. The faint yellow wallpaper (the kind that is painted on with an ornamented roller) appeared to be original, and the smudges, cracks, and orphaned picture hooks were signs of a domestic life fading into memory before our eyes. As we entered the apartment, there was a palpable

sense of continuity with the era in which the Freuds lived in the building—an impression of Vienna in the 1920s and 1930s more vivid than in the renovated spaces of the Freud Museum. During their time at Berggasse 19 the Freuds had, in fact, aspired to move from their apartment into the more grandly proportioned space of their upstairs neighbor, but never had the opportunity.

Rather than renovate the space we decided to preserve the apartment: we could not have asked for a more provocative setting for an exhibition about the couch. Freud's recurring metaphor of analysis as archaeology was echoed in the layered history of the apartment and its claustrophobic domesticity. The concept for the exhibition design was to insert a false floor, heightening the sense of the apartment as an archeological site, a space infused by memory. The exaggerated sound and bright surface of the new floor heightened the sensation of walking through the apartment, dramatizing the contrast between our vertical, waking life and the horizontal dream state of thinking in repose.

The exhibition made a clear demarcation between the "inserted" elements of the design and the existing context of the apartment. This line was articulated through a raised floor that ran throughout the entire space. This white surface signaled that the apartment was as much a part of the "content" of the presentation as the objects on display. A continuous perimeter of light glowed from the gaps between the floor and the walls, providing illumination and defining the point of contact between the exhibition design and the space of the apartment.

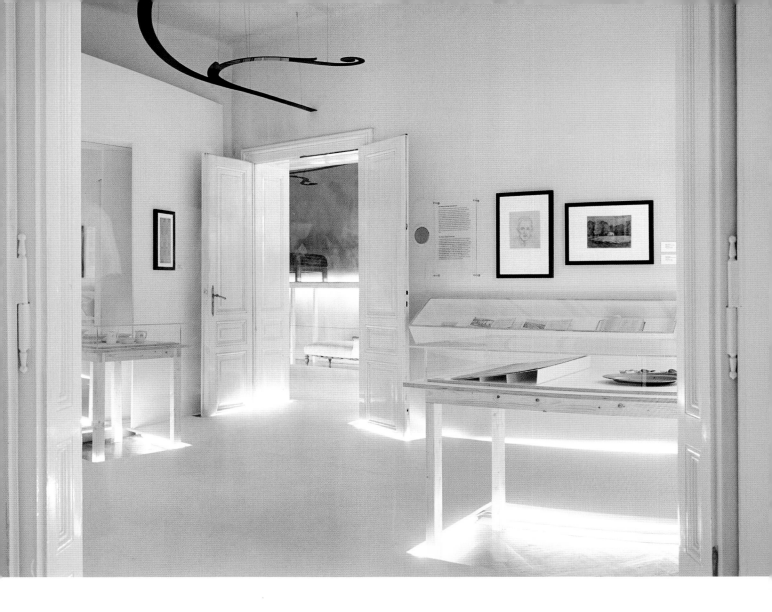

The white floor was cut so that the objects on display, such as Freud's famous writing chair, sat directly on the original parquet flooring—a reversal of the traditional exhibition display technique of placing objects on a pedestal. When raised display surfaces were required, they were created by elevating sections of the floor to become tables and cabinets.

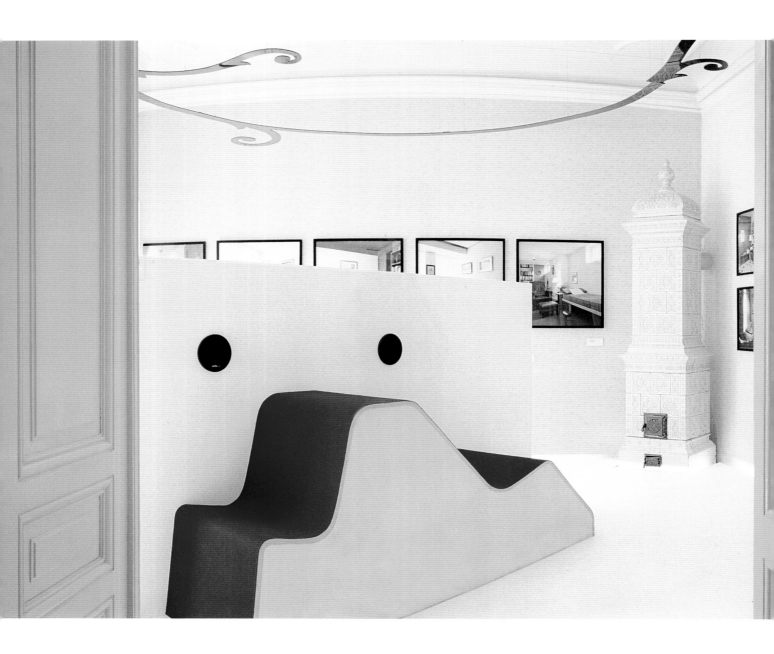

In the parlor a low wall separated two couches on either side. Designed so the analyst and the patient were on the same axis, rather than perpendicular to one another, the couch allowed visitors to sit or recline and listen to analysts reflect on their use of the couch. The walls in the gallery displayed photographs by Shellburne Thurber of couches in analysts' offices in different parts of the world.

ÖSTERREICH 55

DIE COUCH
VOM DENKEN IM LIEGEN

Freud Jahr 2006

ABBOTT MILLER

For a postage stamp to commemorate Freud Year, we adapted the Eames couch silhouette.

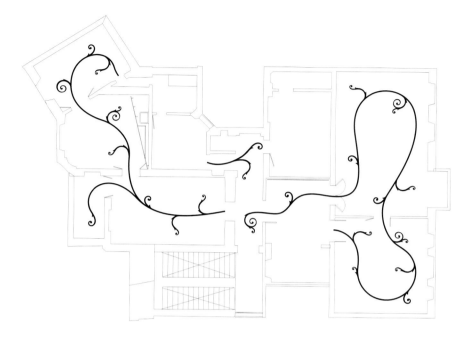

Traversing the space's numerous thresholds, we mapped our story of analytical and therapeutic techniques onto the floor plan and discovered an unusual consonance between the two: in the living room, we received the guest (Freud), in the parlor we staged conversations (with analysts), in the sun porch we discussed light therapy, in the bathroom we explored water therapy, and in the darkest and most claustrophobic spaces of the apartment, we presented techniques of physical control and constraint of the asylum—the flip side of the talking cure.

The apartment's complex layout required navigational cues to indicate the exhibition sequence. A botanical motif etched on the windows in the stairwell inspired the forms of an ornamental device that hung from the ceiling and wound its way through the apartment. The shiny black tendrils hovered over the exhibit and provided a thread through the galleries, as if passing through walls.

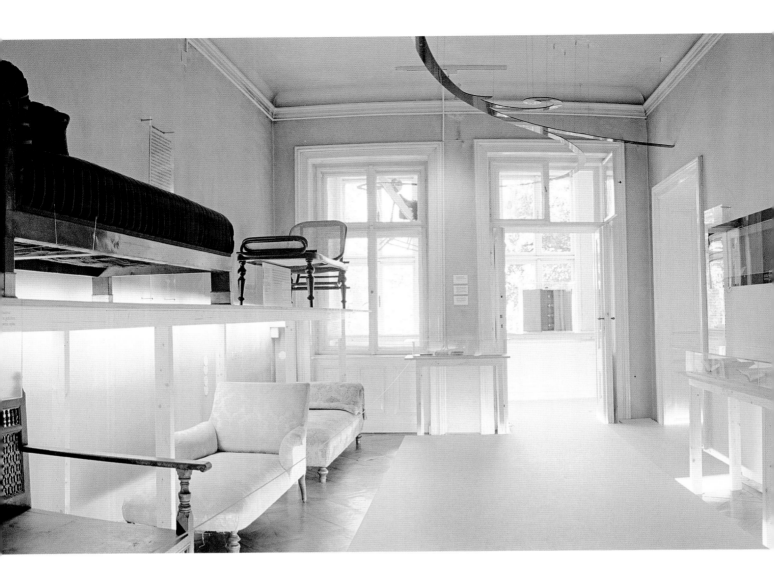

A room devoted to a series of couches and daybeds led to a sun porch with a chaise-lounge that was used at a nearby sanitorium for light therapy treatments.

Draped in a white sheet, Freud's famous couch was shown on the cover of the book as a piece of furniture, but also a corpse at a crime scene. The Freud Museum in London allowed us to drape the mythical object so that the photographer John Ross could capture the couch itself in repose.

An insignia I designed to mark 2006 as "Freud Year" in Austria symbolized its subject in repose, a reference to both the couch and the grave.

Freud Jahr 2006

Sigmund and Martha (2006) was an installation I designed in a street-level exhibition space at the Freud Museum. Over many years the space has featured contemporary artists whose work relates to the ideas or history of psychoanalysis. My project magnified an incidental detail from the correspondence between Freud and Martha Bernays, the woman he would eventually marry.

During their courtship Martha solicited Sigmund's advice on the design of a new monogram she commissioned for her stationery. Among the letters of their almost-daily correspondence Martha sent him a note that featured a letter *B* intertwined with a letter *M*, a recent proposal from the stationer.

The design was unambiguously vertical in orientation, with a traditional haughty grandeur that evoked art nouveau influences.

In his response Freud criticized the monogram: "In my opinion the B on the notepaper is too ostentatious and the M too modest. As you know, I am only interested in the M." In a presumptuous move Freud commissioned a new monogram, which was insistently horizontal. In this small hieroglyph of bourgeois identity, Freud perceived a struggle between ostentation and modesty, between self-aggrandizement and propriety. Their conversation—conducted through the design of the monogram—revealed an intersection of personal and professional

anxieties. Freud's version effectively put Martha's vertical representation on the couch: its forms became voluptuous and fecund as they approached horizontality. This previously obscure contest of hieroglyphs was writ large in the window of the museum—an incidental detail that became a symbol of something more.

the story is the engine

A series of projects designed for Harley-Davidson
provided the opportunity to do large and complex exhibitions with a populist and celebratory
attitude. As a group, these environments show
how an iconic brand provides a strong language
that can respond to diverse contexts, from the
spare white walls of an art museum to the vast
scale of a racetrack. Each project built on insights from the other, allowing me to understand
the culture of the company, the characteristics
of its international audiences, and the visual
and material expressions of Harley-Davidson as
a brand. Conveying the personality of the brand
and capturing the spirit of Harley-Davidson
required an immersion in the company culture,
its archives, and its history. Over the course
of these projects I also came to realize that my
separation from motorcycle culture provided
a valuable perspective. A purely "tribal" approach
can run the risk of presuming too much about
audiences. As a designer you have to be both
"inside" the material and also "outside," in that
you benefit from a certain amount of distance
so you can observe what might be interesting to a
hardcore fan but can still understand the need
to reach uninitiated audiences.

A 2008 poster for a Milwaukee
AIGA lecture on the design
of the Harley-Davidson Museum
suggested that the journey
of a motorcyclist is punctuated
by plate-sized destinations
along the way.

HOG HEAVEN

DESIGNING THE HARLEY-DAVIDSON MUSEUM
THE MEAT AND POTATOES AND THE NUTS AND BOLTS

ABBOTT MILLER, EXHIBITION DESIGNER
JAMES BIBER, ARCHITECT
PENTAGRAM

THE INAUGURAL EVENT OF THE NEWLY FOUNDED
AIGA WISCONSIN CHAPTER

THE HARLEY-DAVIDSON MUSEUM
MILWAUKEE, WISCONSIN
6 PM SEPTEMBER 24, 2008

road show

Harley-Davidson celebrated its centennial with a yearlong Open Road Tour (2002) that traveled to ten cities across the globe. Conceived like a rally, tents and concert stages were set up for a weekend-long event with exhibitions, demonstration rides, musical performances, and stunt and drill cyclists. Due to the scale of the event and the crowds—averaging forty thousand people each day—the festival sites were vast. We united the sprawling site and the different exhibitions through large-scale lettering, monumental imagery, and iconic forms. The project combined the formality of a museum-quality exhibition with the grassroots character of a festival. After traveling to Los Angeles, Atlanta, Baltimore, Toronto, Dallas, Sydney, Tokyo, Barcelona, and Hamburg, the exhibition concluded its tour in Harley's hometown of Milwaukee. At the core of the Machine tent, I designed a typographic tower —a tribute to Futurist poetry—displaying the company's famously named engines: Flathead, Knucklehead, Panhead, Sportster, Shovelhead, Revolution, Twin-Cam, and Evolution.

The project moved with lightning speed and taught me that a seemingly impossible deadline compelled everyone to make decisions quickly and to trust our instincts. This attitude gave the project a sense of clarity and simplicity, which had a positive influence on the overall design.

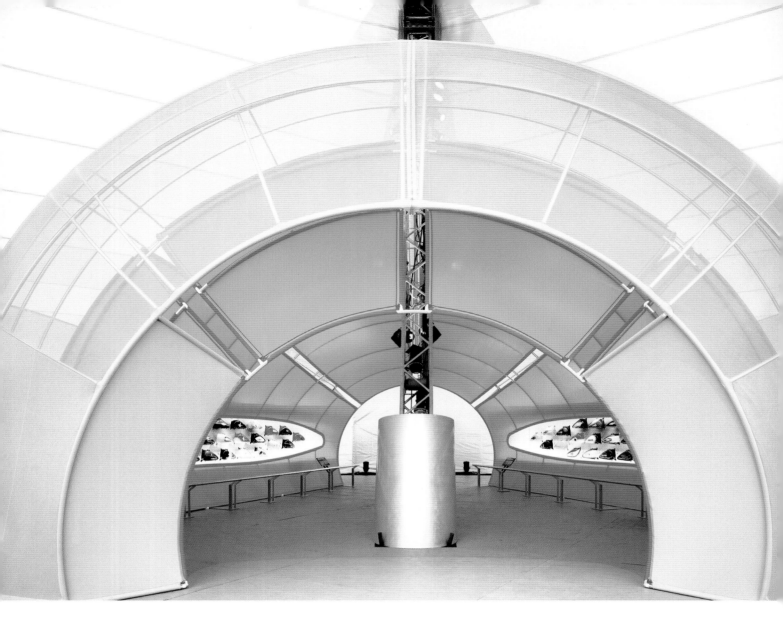

The Open Road Tour embraced the
temporary nature of the event,
using skeletal frameworks, industrial stagecraft, and fabric skins.
We designed an orange fabric tent
to house an exhibition of tanks.
The large tower holding up the tent
was a bare truss clad with eight
telescoping rings of type, which
created an iconic tower. Around its
base we exhibited the actual
engines and housed enormous speakers that played recordings of
the different engines. The roar of
the engines played like the chimes
of a clock, every fifteen minutes.

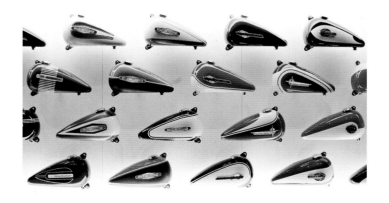

The central tent structure was designed by FTL Happold and built by Canobbio, a circus tent fabricator based in Italy. Within this vast interior we designed modular platforms that recalled segments of roadways that linked together. The structural masts of the tent provided anchors for video footage of iconic rallies around the world.

An exhibition about assembly-line production showed how components are manufactured in different plants and then brought together along a complex assembly sequence. I used the yellow overhead rail system from one of the factories as an armature for images and texts. The elevated text and image panels accommodated the vast crowds that streamed through the exhibition.

Portraits of riders and video testimonials provided a sense of the passionate connection motorcyclists have with Harley-Davidson. Visitors could tape video segments in a photo booth and their contributions were added to the presentation over the course of the tour. A gallery of historic and contemporary photographs conveyed the continuity of riders over the past one hundred years.

Rolling Sculpture: The Art of Harley-Davidson (2003) occupied a Santiago Calatrava–designed pavilion at the Milwaukee Art Museum. The exhibition focused on the design language of Harley-Davidson's styling department. Because the space was so strongly influenced by the architecture—which itself recalls the engineering of roads and bridges—I used the exact form and scale of the concrete ribs of the building, turning them on their sides to become platforms. Using digital files from the original construction documents, we selected three segments of the ribs for the platform vocabulary.

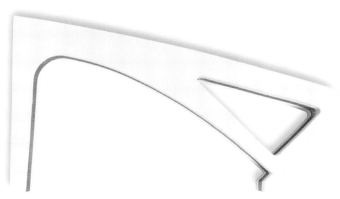

To punctuate the long pavilion we convinced the museum to paint three of the structural ribs in brilliant Harley-Davidson orange. A long table displayed drawings and texts from the styling department.

making a museum

Harley-Davidson had been planning to build a museum for several years when a site in downtown Milwaukee became available. The previous work I'd done with the company on its one hundredth anniversary was solid preparation for designing the permanent exhibitions for the museum. The architect James Biber's design process occurred simultaneously with our exhibition development, which created opportunities for a close fit between the architectural spaces and the exhibition narrative. We worked with curators Jim Fricke and Kristen Jones to gain a sense of the story that could be told through compelling artifacts and images. A combination of thematic and historical galleries allowed us to create different points of focus for different types of visitors. We knew hardcore enthusiasts would savor every detail, but we wanted to address historical, cultural, and design aspects of the story in a way that felt accessible to everyone.

Visitors begin their journey on the second floor, where the entire space of the museum is visible. Motorcycles surge toward visitors on a "road" recessed in the floor on the upper and lower levels, flanked by thematic galleries.

The museum, which opened in 2008, presents a unique hybrid of history museum, science center, and art museum. The exhibition design created different environments within the industrial language of the building so that the presentation felt varied: the reverential mood of the founding years; the more playful presentation of clubs, rallies, and stunt cycling; and a design lab focused on the nature of style and engineering. Our attitude about materials, lighting, color, and three-dimensional form was focused on creating an environment in which the motorcycle's voluptuous forms, polished surfaces, and bursts of intense color had the greatest impact.

As visitors enter the museum, alternate paths are visible: a "road" runs the length of the museum with bridges that cross back and forth. The Engine Room displays the major engine types and provides a tutorial on their components. A long console features an interactive display that allows visitors to explore engine types and hear their sounds.

Photographic imagery is handled in a variety of ways, including printing directly on aluminum wall surfaces and large light boxes. Platforms and railings are minimal and graphic.

A section of boardtrack is built within one gallery: its surface is animated by projections of historic footage from boardtrack races in the years before they were outlawed.

On the following page, galleries devoted to the company history feature a reclaimed wooden factory floor with hints of its former use.

BIG CHANGES
HARD TIMES

Life changed at a dizzying rate during the Roaring Twenties. Women got the vote and movies got sound. Automobiles and household electricity became commonplace. Wages rose and workdays shrank. Mass-produced goods filled the stores, and salesmen offered payment plans to entice consumers to purchase newfangled gadgets like refrigerators, washing machines, and radios.

Harley-Davidson was at the top of the motorcycle business, but the Ford Model T ruled the roads. Tastes changed with the times, however, and by the mid-'20s consumers tired of the old-fashioned Ford and began buying more stylish Chevrolets and Buicks. As a General Motors Styling publication noted, "Appearance and style have assumed equal importance with utility, price, and operation."

The Motor Company, having built its reputation on economy, performance, and reliability, revamped its product line and changed its advertising tactics to remain competitive in this new market. A sophisticated new look and a revolutionary new model kept sales moving through the Great Depression of the 1930s.

ROAD WORK

in the little 10 by 15 factory, turned out three motorcycles. Today there are 1,570 employees. The 1914 output is 20,000, one complete motorcycle every 5 ½ minutes."

The Milwaukee Journal, March 31, 1914

The world seemed to be shrinking as Harley-Davidson entered its second decade. Airplanes were flying longer distances, transforming ideas about travel. The Panama Canal opened, creating new opportunities for intercontinental shipping. Construction began on the Lincoln Highway between New York City and San Francisco, the first transcontinental road in the United States. Drive-in gas stations appeared, and road traffic increased, requiring new controls: Cleveland, Ohio installed the nation's first electric traffic signal. Harley-Davidson had committed dealers all over the United States and began exporting motorcycles around the globe. Maintaining this rate of growth would be challenging, but the company laid a strong foundation for success.

The Service School

The exhibition design creates different zones within the larger volume of the museum. The "road" from the upper level continues on the lower level with a display of the most important pieces in the collection.

A gallery focused on the styling department features prototypes and drawings.

A section of the floor raises up to create a platform for stunt motorcycles. Video monitors on the underside of the platform display footage of stunt riders.

identity links pixels and bricks

I hate logos. Why? Because everyone gets obsessed with the logo when they should really be more concerned with how it's used. I have designed many logos, but I approach them not as the most important component of a graphic identity, but as the most succinct expression of that identity. A logo is what can be deployed, consistently, in the absence of all other signifiers. A logo is an inherently reductive proposition, which is why I like them to have the simplicity of a word—something not much more complicated than a typographic construction. Perhaps this is why so many marks I've designed bear the traces of an architectural or figurative reference, something that relates back to its origin in the physical specificity of a place.

Graphic identity is the adhesive that connects physical and digital experience. To be effective across multiple contexts, a graphic identity needs to establish a succinct vocabulary of elements that can be rendered in different scales, materials, and media. Unlike the design of a book, which is complete once it is published, a graphic identity program depends on the energy and talent that goes into its future success. Some elements are designed at the outset of the project, as part of the initial wave of establishing a new identity: publications, signage, and merchandise. Institutions and businesses invest in the "tool kit" of a graphic identity, but they need to stay vigilant and engaged to keep it running, reevaluate its performance and maintain it, just as a physical building must be maintained. An identity can only be effective when it keeps its vitality and consistency in the face of constant change and use. Beyond the core elements of a logo, typefaces, and colors, a graphic identity needs enough development to translate it into a sensibility about its materiality, its literary "voice," and its overall personality.

M|I|C/A

MICA, officially known as the Maryland Institute College of Art, straddles a major boulevard in Baltimore. The historic Main Building of 1907, which looks as if it were carved from a giant chunk of white marble, is situated directly across from the 2003 Brown Center, a taut glass iceberg of a building that projects over the street as if nodding to its older colleague. In creating a graphic identity for the school I wanted to capture its juxtaposition of historical and modern sensibilities, and to specifically reference the dialogue between the two buildings.

Founded in 1826, the school is one of the oldest art schools in the nation, evident in its turn-of-the-century buildings and campus. The wordmark we developed in 2007 is a typographic portrait of this relationship: the monumental capitals are seen in counterpoint to the rhythm of fine verticals, the last of which carries the angled "prow" of the Brown Center facade. A pattern within the identity program recalls the ornamental motifs and mosaics of the Main Building, as well as the fritted pattern of dots on all of the panels in the Brown Center. A book we designed to recognize the school's 175th anniversary used dots silkscreened on vellum to simulate the pointillist rendering that occurs when looking from the Brown Center to the Main Building.

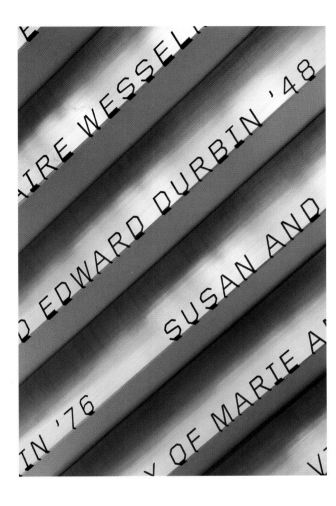

Cooper Union commissioned
a building by Morphosis in 2008,
adjacent to the historic 1858
Foundation Building on Cooper
Square. As a student at Cooper
I was intrigued by the block
lettering above the entrance to
the Foundation Building that
identifies the school and heroically
declares "To Science and Art."
Like letters on technical drawings,
diagrams, and blueprints, their
t-square and triangle forms suggest
the school's nineteenth-century
origins. In our environmental graphics we use Wim Crouwel's 1974
font Gridnik, which follows the spirit
of the historic block letters but in
a more modern voice.

Because of its geometric clarity, Gridnik retains a consistency of expression across varying scales, materials, and techniques: on the previous pages it is twisted and punched through the facade's canopy and etched on steel fins above a stairwell. At right, it forms stripes like a bar code as it turns a corner. Below, it's engraved in concrete pavers that stretch across a roof terrace.

The Noguchi Museum is a perfectly distilled expression of artist Isamu Noguchi's work. He created the museum in his Long Island City studio as a permanent record of his work, which included sculpture, furniture, and gardens. In designing a graphic identity and environmental graphics in 2004, I wanted to reference his use of organically inflected geometries. One of my favorite fonts, Balance by Evert Bloemsma, features gently concave edges that recall the carved and cast surfaces and silhouettes of Noguchi's work. The identity and signage use this subtle concave language with a simple black-and-white palette.

The Guggenheim Museum invited me to design a new magazine for its members in 1996. I proposed that we develop the Frank Lloyd Wright lettering on their famous facade into a typeface that could become the basis for the magazine and, eventually, the signature of the museum. Working with type designer Jonathan Hoefler, the font now known as Verlag has become the *lingua franca* of the global Guggenheim network, used prominently in our design of the website and on all communications. A book we designed on the history of the building used the font in a circular composition that recalls the vertiginous space inside the rotunda. I've worked with the museum, one of my earliest clients, on many projects over the last two decades. A dream project of mine is to design an exhibition in the rotunda—I just thought I'd put that out there and see if anyone at the Guggenheim wants to make my dream come true.

GUGGENHEIM

**ART
INSTITVTE
CHICAGO**

The Art Institute of Chicago faces Michigan Avenue with a regal set of stairs flanked by two sculptural lions, capped by a frieze inscribed with the name of the museum and the names of famous artists the museum hoped, at its founding, to eventually display. The use of a Roman *v* in the word *Institute* nods to the classical past and the notion of the art-museum-as-temple. These classical antecedents are also at play in the new Modern Wing designed by Renzo Piano. Our graphic identity and signage program links the historic building with the Modern Wing through lettering that fuses modern and classical sensibilities. Topaz, a contemporary display typeface by Jonathan Hoefler, was curiously well matched to the spirit of the carved letters in the original Michigan Avenue frieze. We commissioned Hoefler to expand Topaz into a full typeface, called Ideal Sans, that could be used on signage and in all print and digital communications. Piano's careful orchestration of stone and glass throughout the addition provided opportunities to integrate the lettering in ways that echoed the monumental character of the Michigan Avenue facade.

MIHO
美学院

The Miho Institute of Aesthetics
is a newly founded school in Japan,
located an hour north of Kyoto.
Nestled in a forested landscape, it is
part of a campus of buildings that
includes the Miho Museum—an
extraordinary art collection displayed
in a series of pavilions designed
by I.M. Pei. The school buildings and
landscape were designed by io
Architects and completed in 2012.

The identity I developed for the
school features a symbol based
on the distinctive shape of a wall
relief in the Miho collection. The
form alludes to the image of an open
book and the top of a pen or brush.
Its steeply tapered forms also recall
the silhouette of a bell tower on the
campus, designed by Pei.

The symbol was integrated into
a number of architectural features,
including door handles, metal
screens, and shoji screens in a tea-
house. The stage curtain we designed
was handwoven in silk by a team
of artisans working on an enormous
loom for five months—the most
lovingly and expensively produced
object I've ever designed.

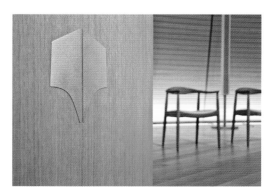

HOMEROOM 1B

308

A channel of skylights floods the hallways with natural light that washes down the walls leading into classrooms. A halo of colored light is created by brilliant colors applied to the back of the signs. Exterior directional signs are connected to columns. At night the letters glow from within the lanterns.

ク GYMNASIUM・LIBRARY
体育館・図書館

WILLIAM JOHN HENNESSY

SEYMOUR JOSEPH GUY   JOHN AUGUSTUS HO

GEORGE HENRY SMILLIE   JOHN FER

ENOCH WOOD PERRY JR.   PLATT

JAMES HOPE   WILLIAM MORRIS HUM

CHARLES HENRY MILLER   ALFRED WORDS

WALTER SATTERLEE   **1880**   ANDREW

1883   HARRY CHASE   FREDERICK S

WILMER DEWING   FREDERICK WARREN FREE

WELDON   IRVING RAMSAY WILES   **189**

BEAUX   HARRY WILLSON WATROUS   WIL

MEDLEY   ROBERT WARD VAN BOSKERCK

WILLIAM VONNOH   **1900**   SAMUEL ISHAM

AROLD DAVIS   CHARLES WARREN EATON

WILLIAM GEDNEY BUNCE   THOMA

PHILIP MARTINY   CHARLES HENRY NIEHA

CHARLES TARBELL   **1905**   FREDERIC CROWIN

ARDINER CUSHING   JAMES FRANCIS DAY

DORA WHEELER KEITH   ISIDORE K

The National Academy was America's first art museum and art school. It was founded in 1826 by a group of artists who wanted to echo European academies, which taught and displayed art for the general public. The elected members form an incredible list of artists and architects central to American art. The academy has occupied a historic mansion on Fifth Avenue since 1942 that was renovated in 2011. I revised the "NA" mark and developed a system based on the typeface Plan by Peter Bil'ak. A dramatic ceiling in the lobby features the names of over two thousand academy members and the years they were elected. Architects Bade Stageberg Cox created a jewel-like space in which the white-on-white "cloud" of names hovers above. This ongoing roll call of members is routed in Corian with an academy-red infill on dates.

FOUNDED IN 1825, THE NATIONAL ACADEMY IS THE ONLY INSTITUTION OF ITS KIND THAT INTEGRATES A MUSEUM, ART SCHOOL, AND ASSOCIATION OF ARTISTS AND ARCHITECTS DEDICATED TO CREATING AND PRESERVING A LIVING HISTORY OF AMERICAN ART.

THE BARNES FOUNDATION

The Barnes Foundation was established by Albert C. Barnes in 1927 as an institution to advance the appreciation and study of art. Having amassed a fortune from his work as a chemist, Barnes devoted his life to art and created a gallery to display his collection—paintings by Cezanne, Van Gogh, Matisse, and old masters. Visitors were admitted for courses and lectures, witnessing an ongoing experiment in the display of art. Barnes was interested in the visual dialogue between works in his collection: his installation strategy consisted of what he called "ensembles"—axially symmetrical compositions that, on close inspection, reveal conversations among the works displayed, whether through subject, composition, form, color, or texture. Barnes also displayed African art, furniture, and decorative ironwork as equally valid participants in these ensembles.

In creating the graphic identity, website, books, and signage for the Barnes, for its relocation to downtown Philadelphia in 2012, I emphasized the role of the ensemble in the experience of the collection. The architecture of the new building replicates the exact proportions of the original galleries but situates them within an elegant sequence of stone-clad volumes designed by Tod Williams Billie Tsien Architects. The environmental graphics follow the serene materiality of the spaces and insert reminders of Barnes's presence among the treasures.

ANY WORK OF ART. DR. ALBERT BARNES, 1925

A pool of water near the entrance is edged with a quote from Barnes expressing the integrity of all art, whether a painting, a poem, or a symphony. At right, the signature, in the typeface Milo by Mike Abbink, is rendered in steel letters against the stone facade.

On the following page, a garden wall features a graphic translation of a 1927 letter from Barnes with notations for the display of several new paintings he acquired. The gestural character of his handwriting is captured in the twisted forms of wrought iron, connecting with Barnes's ongoing interest in decorative metalwork.

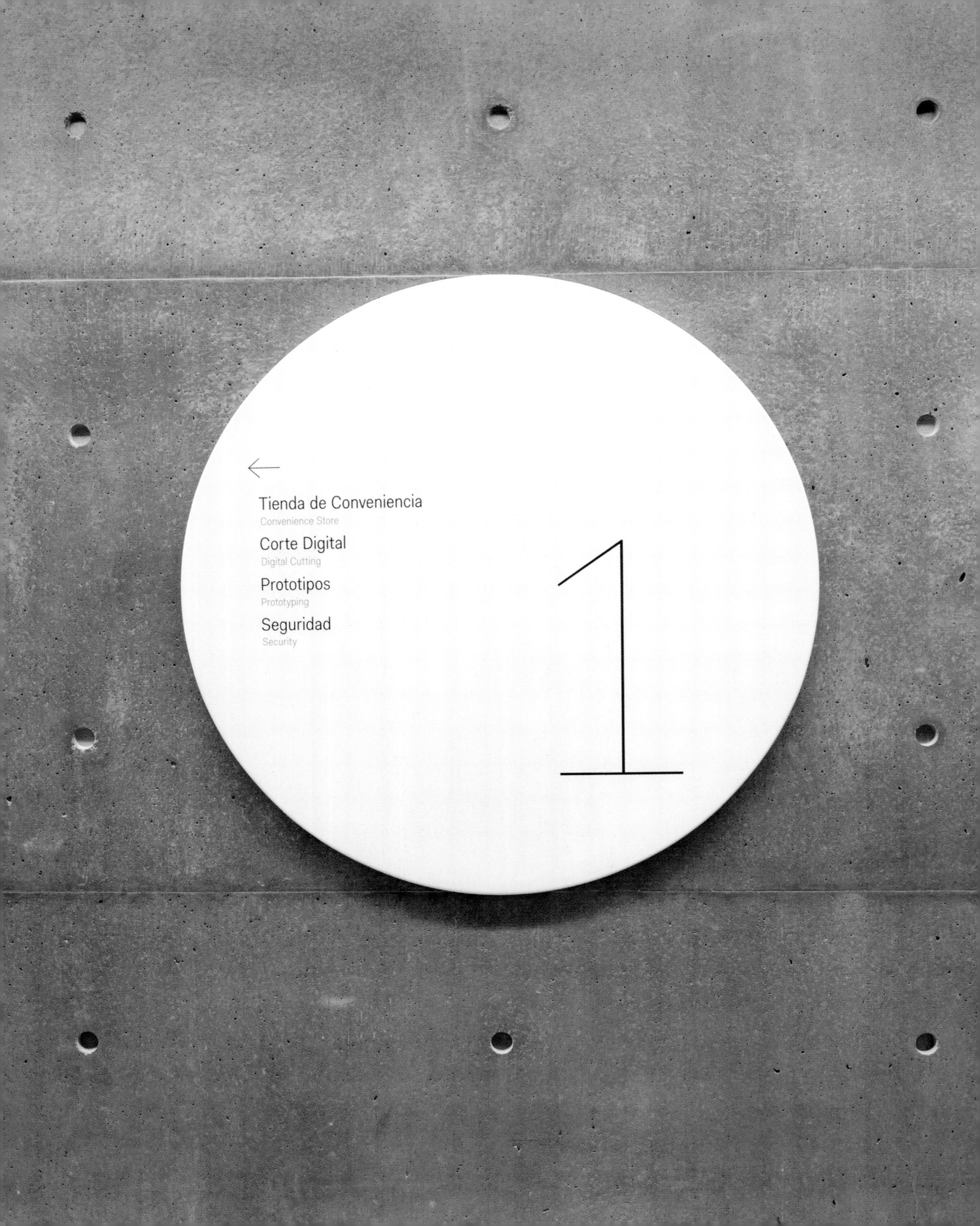

←

Tienda de Conveniencia
Convenience Store

Corte Digital
Digital Cutting

Prototipos
Prototyping

Seguridad
Security

1

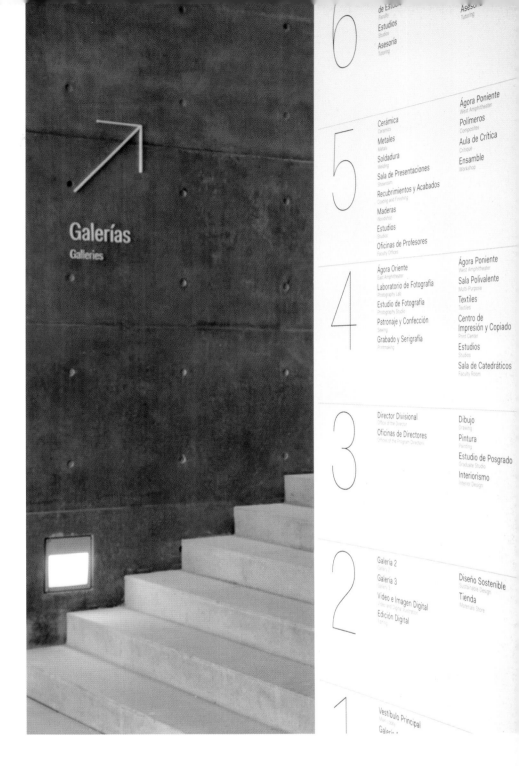

Universidad de Monterrey is a leading university located in a mountainous landscape of Monterrey, in northeast Mexico. We designed a graphic identity and signage for a new center for art and design on the campus, housed in a dramatic building designed by Tadao Ando. The monumental concrete building rises up out of the mountains and provides amazing vistas of the region. Signage within the Ando building takes a contrarian approach: pristine white lettering, glossy white discs, and glassy prisms form a counterpoint to the rough gray concrete walls. The sign family consists of discs in various scales, ranging from six-inch diameter to five feet. The typeface used throughout the environmental graphics is Fakt, designed by Thomas Thiemich.

GI & A SERVICIOS LEGALES, S.C.
CONSTRUCTORA GARZA PONCE S.A. DE C.V.
ANONIMO
SR. JESUS HERRERA GUTIERREZ
ALEJANDRA DOMINGUEZ DE FERNANDEZ

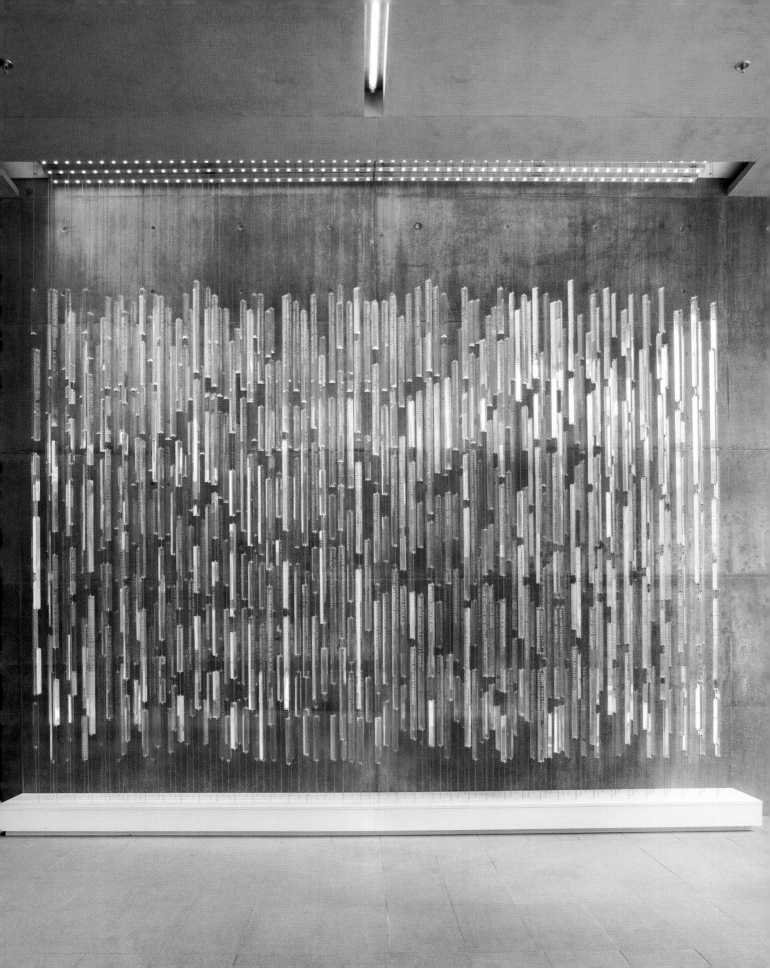

Spreads from *Cover to Cover*
by Michael Snow, 1975

the idea is the machine

Why is "design" synonymous with stylistic progress? The focus on the aesthetic development of design has served to make false distinctions between good and bad, progressive and reactionary, new and old. Other criteria—ranging from legibility and function to language and ecology—have tempered the search for style, yet overwhelmingly, designers judge design in terms of its contribution to a legacy of formal invention. The imperative of stylistic renewal has progressed to such an extent that today a "look" can run its course in a few months.

Since the 1980s, designers have expressed increasing anxiety about the degree to which the field has become a style industry or fashion system. The way the cutting edge repeatedly becomes a favorite tool for commercial and corporate interests proves that radical style can be incorporated, recuperated, and neutralized. The speed of this innovation/absorption cycle has accelerated, but no more so than in films, clothing, or music. Designers respond to the phenomenon with a range of emotions from pleasure to disgust. Yet whether it is embraced or despised, stylistic innovation is the framework within which design is commonly judged.

The succession of styles championed by annuals, competitions, and design magazines is not the only way to view design. Another perspective sees design as a structural language made up of the typographic and pictorial conventions of publishing, advertising, journalism and entertainment. In contrast to the Modernist ideal of a universal, transhistorical language of vision (point, line, plane), the language of media is rooted in modes of communication that are culturally specific—they are, in fact, fundamental to modern Western culture.

recycling structure

Shifting the focus from style to structure loosens the grip of chronology, affording a glimpse of relationships between historically divergent practices. For instance, the device of framing a text to look like a book-within-a-book recurs across the history of design. This structure dates back to manuscript and incunabula traditions in which a central text is framed by a commentary. While the structure has been recycled at different points in history, the book-within-a-book is an "idea" and a structure that remains independent of particular instances of its use. Artist Barbara Bloom's book *The Reign of Narcissism* consists of a sequence of facsimile-style spreads resting within an otherwise traditional book. The shift in scale and the photographic depth of the pages force the viewer to see the page as an image.

Other examples use the book-within-a-book structure for both its pictorial and conceptual value. The French philosopher Jacques Derrida exploited the spatial and typographic resources of the page to find ways of writing that are not reducible to verbal form. For his 1974 *Glas*, he drew on the intricate textual "glosses" in medieval books and the framed commentary of the Talmud as models of nonlinear, polyphonic texts. Traditionally, the Hebrew-Aramaic text of the Talmud is surrounded by interpretations, translations, and notes. In *Glas*, Derrida places two texts next to one another on the same page: in the left column is an analysis of Hegel, while on the right he makes a series of observations on Genet through a web of puns and alliteration.

These citations of the book-within-a-book structure are not "timeless" or "universal," for each bears the aesthetic marks of its time. They refer to a design convention but are not stylistic quotations. Instead, a visual form is employed more for its structure than for its style.

The "vernacular" has become a familiar breeding ground of ideas for graphic designers, but here the closed loop of imitation and appropriation has become hackneyed and condescending, positioning the designer as a cultural tourist.

A different relationship to historical sources involves apprehending such forms as conceptual models rather than as stock imagery. Such an approach borrows the principle behind an artifact rather than its surface manifestation. Principles are not proprietary in the same way as a designer's stylistic signature: structure does not have an obvious historical starting point in the same way as stylistic forms do. Making use of a principle does not necessarily entail mimicry.

All design has structure: in the case of books, for example, structure consists of the "software" of the page (sequence, margins, running heads, body copy, footnotes) and the hardware of the physical object (cover, paper, folding, binding). Some design actively engages structure, making visible the otherwise transparent conventions. What is used automatically by one designer—a two-column grid, for example—may be used actively or critically by another who sets up an explicit relationship between the two columns.

Fred Struving's design for the 1989 book *Photography Between Covers: The Dutch Documentary Photobook*

After 1945 uses the left column for the Dutch text and the right for the English translation. The wide space between the two accommodates footnotes for both texts, which are set flush left and right respectively. Quotations also indent and outdent, so their ragged edges meet in the space between columns. Most of the photographic material in the book runs across the bottom of the page. This inventive format brings materials usually placed in the margins to the center and situates the illustrations in a position ordinarily reserved for notes. Such an approach—introspective, studious, subtle—investigates the traditions of the page and shows how the practice of design may constitute a form of research.

effacing the designer

While a structural view of design does not dictate an aesthetic program, an interest in foregrounding structure often leads to a minimal approach that effaces the "hand" of the designer. Experimental filmmaker and artist Michael Snow's 1975 book *Cover to Cover* eliminates all text, allowing the narrative to unfold through a sequence of photographs. Snow dramatizes structure by making the turning of the page signify the opening of a door or the passage of time, exploiting the momentary eclipse of vision that occurs as one page replaces the next. Snow's book recalls Renaissance title pages that use architectural "entrances" as the reader's point of entry to a book.

This approach to structure entails an allegiance to the resources of the medium, an investment in achieving maximum expressive potential from a given system. Thus while style and decoration are additive, structure comes from within the medium, generating form from the inside out.

typology and pattern

Approaching design through the filter of structure has affinities with the artistic practices of Sol LeWitt and other conceptual and process artists of the 1960s and 1970s. LeWitt's wall drawings were executed from a series of verbal descriptions. His famous statement that "The idea is the machine that makes art" holds true for design that lets form unfold from structure.

The fascinations of the Dadaists and Surrealists with "readymade" objects—the ordinary form placed in a different context and pressed into the service of an alternative function—is another important source for design. A 1992 catalogue for a Dutch exhibition about

Duchamp performed a reflexive use of the readymade within graphic design. The first half of *Al(l)ready Made* includes essays and color photographs of works of art featured in the exhibition, while the second half is a commercially produced diary for 1993. The book as a whole embraces the format and production techniques of the diary, including its faux leather grain cover and gold embossed lettering.

Because structure is operative in all forms of textual production—because it is in essence public domain—many examples of a structuralist approach by nondesigners can be found. Wilbur Schramm's 1959 book *One Day in the World's Press* charts the global response to two major events that took place on November 2, 1956: the Soviet Army's second invasion of Hungary and the attack on Egypt by British and French allied naval forces. *One Day in the World's Press* provides a simultaneous view of the events from fourteen newspapers from Europe, Africa, Asia and South America, which are translated into English and reconfigured as facsimile reproductions.

Rather than simply producing an annotated translation, Schramm preserved the relationship between elements in the original layouts. Schramm's method reveals the hierarchical structure of media, showing the grid of the newspaper to be an active agent in the construction of meaning. The Schramm project enacts a comparative analysis of "layout" and the power of newspapers to configure reality. By viewing the refraction of these stories through different national perspectives, *One Day in the World's Press* implicitly critiques the notions of one "true" account.

Illustrator and writer Leanne Shapton's 2009 book *Important Artifacts and Personal Property from the Collection of Lenore Doolan and Harold Morris, Including Books, Street Fashion, and Jewelry* cleverly and obliquely tells the story of a romantic relationship that has unraveled. Employing the literary, typographic, Zand visual conventions of an auction catalogue, the narrative emerges from three hundred twenty-five "lot descriptions" that detail the physical traces of their relationship (a tee shirt, a mug, a photograph) in much the same way that auction catalogues use historical and biographical information to fetishize an object.

Martin Venezky's design for *The Designer as Author, Producer, Activist, Entreprenuer, Curator and Collaborator: New Models for Communicating*, a book by Steven McCarthy, employs a recurring design strategy born of the Google-era. Whenever a person, place, or artifact is

Spread from Jacques Derrida's
Glas, designed by Richard
Eckersley, University of Nebraska
Press, 1986

*Photography Between Covers:
The Dutch Documentary
Photobook After 1945*, designed
by Fred Struving, 1989

Spread from Barbara Bloom's
The Reign of Narcissism,
Serpentine Gallery, London, 1990

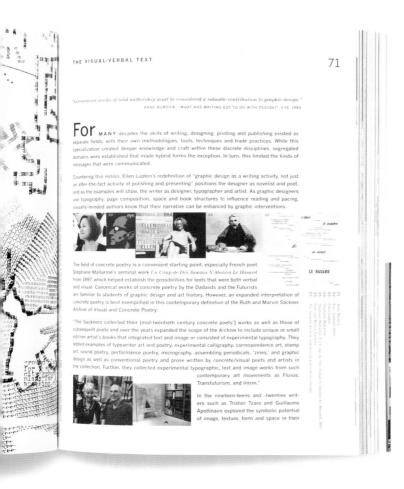

Spread from Steven McCarthy's *The Designer as Author, Producer, Activist, Entreprenuer, Curator, and Collaborator: New Models for Communicating*, 2013. Design by Martin Venezky's Appetite Engineers.

Spread from Erving Goffman's *Gender Advertisements*, 1979

Spread from *Important Artifacts and Personal Property from the Collection of Lenore Doolan and Harold Morris, Including Books, Street Fashion, and Jewelry*, by Leanne Shapton, 2009

referred to in the text, small images from internet searches on the subject are incorporated within the layout of the text. Like a form of visual Tourette Syndrome, the small eruption of icons suggest an erosion of the hierarchy between texts and images—perhaps even an erosion of what constitutes a "useful" image. The untethered, low-resolution images that wash ashore on the internet are accommodated as awkward guests (some are awkward, many are welcome as visual footnotes and marginalia!) within the structure of Venezky's design.

Typologies—the repeated patterns of a genre—are central to the consideration of structure in design. A project which takes repeated patterns as its subject is sociologist Erving Goffman's prescient 1979 book *Gender Advertisements*. Goffman takes an anthropological view of advertising and journalism, analyzing the recurrence of poses, facial expressions, and relationships between figures. Pages are divided into sections that group a series of poses, such as snuggling, sitting, and finger-to-mouth. Goffman's layout provides what the information designer Edward Tufte has called "small multiples": a finely textured array of units that enables the eye to scan quickly for differences and similarities. *Gender Advertisements* precedes the works of artists such as Cindy Sherman and Barbara Kruger, who investigate media as a reservoir of poses that speak about the social construction of gender and sexuality. While Goffman's book is crudely designed, its author has devised a way of writing with pictures, reversing the traditional dominance of text in academic projects.

design as public language

Gender Advertisements presents the repeated structures of photographic language, but there are also a vast range of recurrent typographic and compositional structures in design that form the subject of many "how-to" manuals. Don May's 1942 book *101 Roughs: A Handbook of Advertising Layout* describes its ambition to "classify the physical appearance of printed advertisements into thirty-one patterns...very much like one would collect styles of lettering." In a series of pencil sketches, May provides an inventory of compositional possibilities, giving schematic illustrations of relationships between text and images. Some of May's categories—"oblique," "vertical," or "center axis," for example—are straightforward; others, such as the "eclipse," whereby the copy is positioned "in a panel over a portion of the illustration" are more idiosyncratic.

Such pragmatic books, many of them identified with the "low" culture of advertising, may seem lightweight against the example of more sophisticated design treatises. But commercial layout books from the 1920s to the 1950s are more than amusing relics. Many of these books offer sophisticated typologies, suggesting that we should uncouple the concept of the "vernacular" from notions of naivete or, conversely, the idea that commercial layout was practiced in a rigid, formulaic fashion.

Investigating structure divests design of its focus on the "signature" of the designer and looks instead at design as a public language. Apart from specialized audiences who have an awareness of how designers shape communication, design is a largely anonymous activity. "Design without designers" surrounds us in all forms of institutional, educational, governmental, and commercial media. Post-structuralist writers such as Michel Foucault and Roland Barthes critiqued the humanist ideal of the "individual" as a unified, self-knowing subject. For instance, Foucault examined the way privacy, sexuality, hygiene, and mental health are shaped by the controlling structure of schools, hospitals, and factories. Foucault, like the others, moved from the humanist subject as the authorial source of individuality to the social contexts that make up modern individuality.

The incorporation of post-structuralist theory into design programs and design journalism in the 1980s and 1990s softened the anti-humanist dimension of much post-structuralist thinking. Theory has been used as another way of grinding the same axe: deconstruction has turned into deconstructivism; a critical tool is turned into the name of a style. The post-structuralist project is critical of intuition, self-expression, originality, and self-determination—notions contemporary design take at face value.

Looking at structure offers a way to loosen design from the grip of individuality and chronology (which both boil down to style). A structural view reconfigures the formal, historical, and conceptual terrain of graphic design. Instead of locating an example of design along a stylistic continuum, a structuralist view slices the pie differently, looking at design as a cross section of the vast media of text and image production. Looking at structure—typographic, compositional, institutional, or historical—complicates the rules of the game because structure is about the rules of the game.

First published in *Eye* Vol. 3, No. 10 (Autumn 1993)

Textile Field, designed by Ronan
and Erwan Bouroullec, Victoria
and Albert Museum, London, 2011

from object to observer

Exhibition design deals with the disposition of objects in space: their conceptual and physical relationship to one another and to the observer. Coordinating this complex interaction makes the exhibition designer a choreographer—of objects, images, texts, and people. How we behave in an exhibition, what we feel permitted to do, and how we interact with what is on display are all aspects of design. Exhibitions blend the complex factors of architectural space with the narrative concerns of book and magazine design.

From early cabinets of curiosity to the modern museum, techniques for presenting objects and images—frames, pedestals, vitrines, and dioramas—have developed into a codified repertoire. In the 1920s, the European avant-garde reinvigorated the language of exhibitions by shifting the emphasis from staging the object to staging the observer.

Whereas traditional exhibitions had assumed an idealized and disembodied viewer, avant-garde designers were captivated by the idea of a dynamic observer: one drawing by Herbert Bayer represented a figure in an exhibition with a large eyeball replacing the head on a body. Positioned on a platform and enveloped by angled planes, the eye-body is a vivid illustration of the modernist desire to both expand the field of vision and situate the body in space and time. Both Bayer and Walter Gropius would employ these techniques in their work on exhibitions in Europe and the United States, establishing angled, floating graphic planes as one of the dominant tropes of modern exhibition design.

Among avant-garde designers, new attitudes and forms in exhibition design followed directly from developments in painting, sculpture, graphics, film, and architecture. In the groundbreaking work of El Lissitzky—who considered exhibition design to be his most important contribution—the viewer is both subject and object. In 1927, the visionary museum director Alexander Dorner invited Lissitzky to create a contemporary art room at the Landesmuseum in Hanover, Germany. Lissitzky covered the walls with colored wooden strips, creating different effects as visitors moved through the gallery. Lissitzky's 1928 Pressa exhibition brought photomontage techniques to exhibition design, dissolving the boundaries between the physical space and the more abstract space of photography and mass media.

Frederick Kiesler's landmark 1924 Exhibition of New Theater Techniques in Vienna allowed visitors to adjust the height and viewing angle of works on display.

Kiesler named the system "L and T" based on its modular, typographic construction; it helped inaugurate the skeletal and modular approach that underlies much exhibition design to this day. What made it both radical and influential was the way it treated the exhibition system as an entity independent of its architectural setting—an abstract sculptural event in space. The project, with its responsiveness to the observer's manipulation, marked an early, radical rethinking of the relationship between object and observer, making that relationship reciprocal and malleable.

In today's context, the heritage of both "conventional" techniques and modernist strategies coexist. Designers must stay attuned to the importance of staging the object, but the ambition to stage the observer demands a wider frame of reference, one concerned with the total experience of the viewer/reader, and a broader context of interpretation. These strategies can engage the audience and dramatize their encounter with original artifacts to make visitors see them in a different way, or they can create a context for ideas in the absence of compelling artifacts.

A powerful example of how design can recontextualize and deepen the viewers' experience is Textile Field, a 2011 installation by Ronan and Erwan Bouroullec for the Victoria and Albert Museum (V&A) in London. The designers were invited to create a project that would engage the V&A's existing galleries. They chose the famous Raphael Gallery, which features massive cartoons created as studies for tapestries in the Sistine Chapel. Whereas the tilting planes of avant-garde exhibition design created dynamic angles on which to display objects and graphics, the Bouroullec installation used tilted planes to stage the viewer in relation to the artwork. The installation's vast field with sloping sides invited visitors to sit and lie down to view the artwork, fundamentally changing the character of the space from the more narrow conventions of museum display. In an interview the designers commented on their intention to change the way people interact with art. "The challenge was to invent or define something that could put people in a different situation, that is, to think about it as though it were an interiors project: if it's successful from an ergonomic point of view, if it's comfortable, and if it makes users feel at ease, even psychologically. We began to imagine a swimming pool in this great hall and then a sandy beach where you can lie down and admire a landscape."[1]

Textile Field altered the spatial, physical relationship of the viewer to the work of art, establishing different possibilities that affected their viewing perspective, their behavior, and the duration of their experience. If Textile Field represents an open-ended platform of contemplation—free of specific goals and educational agendas—an exhibition at the Maritime Museum in Stockholm represented the other extreme of a highly choreographed experience. Designers Per Bornstein and Mattias Lind of the Swedish firm White Architects created an installation of maritime paintings so that the horizon lines of the paintings formed a consistent datum through the installation.

Visitors standing at the center of the gallery were enveloped by a 360-degree expanse of sea and ships. As they stray from that central point, the composition splinters into an array of facets. The paintings floated in a sea of blackness, hung on freestanding supports that paradoxically foregrounded their materiality as objects while heightening the illusion of a panoramic vista. The installation dramatized the continuity of sea and sky, rendering individual works as part of an ongoing dialogue with the ocean. As observers moved in closer to the paintings and strayed from the center point (marked by a red light projected on the floor) the singular impression of the collection gave way to the impact of individual paintings. The installation modulated between object and observer, providing moments when individual objects moved to the fore-ground and other times when the "story" narrowed down to the observer's perspective within the gallery.

A similar transformation is evident in an exhibition by the artist Barbara Bloom at the Museum of Applied Arts (MAK) in Vienna. The museum invited a group of artists to work with curators at MAK to create a series of permanent installations. Bloom's subject consisted of an array of fin de siècle bentwood furniture from the Thonet company. Her installation lined a long gallery with a parade of Thonet pieces—a visual essay on the profusion of stylistic effects of the bentwood tech-nique. The beauty of the installation consists in the way Bloom positioned the furniture behind two long scrims, showing the cast shadows of the objects. The installation gave us diagram and silhouette first, with the full three-dimensional experience available only after walking behind the scrim. It is a powerful example of how design can foreground aspects of a collection and create a narrative sequence through the act of disclosure. The shadow view heightened the experience, making the observer focus on its most salient properties by withholding information.

Exhibition designers and curators often describe their work as storytelling, but some stories can be told through objects and images more easily than others. The British design firm Casson Mann has created several ambitious narrative exhibitions that have set a new standard for the way artifacts, texts, and interactivity can be woven into a complex whole. Because exhibi-tions are such a hybrid form—involving architecture, industrial design, graphics, and interaction design—it is easy to lose the physical and editorial continuity of a story, as visitors encounter so much information delivered through many different media.

One aspect that sets Casson Mann's work apart is a synthetic integration of these elements—all the more noteworthy because the firm collaborates with different disciplinary specialists. Graphic designer Nick Bell worked with Casson Mann on the Winston Churchill Museum at the Cabinet War Rooms in London, as well as on the Sellafield Visitors Centre. Bell's typography and media work, which is itself remarkable in the context of exhibitions, but in Casson Mann's work there is a deeper acknowledgment of graphic design in the density of information presented, often employing the compositional strategies of books and magazines. Objects and images are tightly edited and then given space to breathe.

Interactive elements are also skillfully woven into the fabric of Casson Mann's exhibitions. In the Churchill Museum, various tablet-like screens were dispersed throughout, featuring simple, short exercises that attracted children and adults. The centerpiece was an enormous touch-screen table, developed in collab-oration with Bell and designer David Small. The table is given a commanding central space within the museum, cutting a dramatic diagonal through the exhibitions. It presented a series of virtual files that, when touched, opened to reveal texts and photographs that moved deeper into the history of World War II. Several visitors could work independently at the table, but occasion-ally the entire surface was affected by the opening of one of the "files." In these moments the individual activities of visitors were disrupted by a communal experience, such as a rocket that blasted from one end of the table to the other. The table became a kind of bedrock of detail, effectively hinting at the depth of material that curators and exhibition designers feel a responsibility to present.

Between Hägg & Sillén, designed by Per Bornstein and Mattias Lind of the Swedish firm White Architects, The Maritime Museum, Stockholm, 2003. Photograph by Johan Fowelin, courtesy of White Architects.

An installation of Thonet's bentwood furniture, designed by Barbara Bloom, Museum of Applied Arts (MAK), Vienna, 1994. Photograph by Gerald Zugmann.

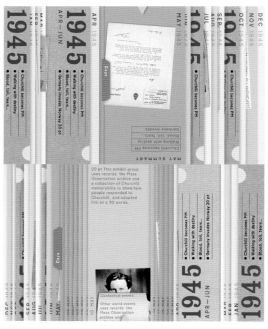

Churchill Museum, designed by Casson Mann, Cabinet War Rooms at the Imperial War Museum, London, 2005. The software and interaction design was developed by David Small. Photographs by John Maclean. Exhibition graphics: Nick Bell Design. Lifeline Table software: Small Design Firm.

Sparking Reaction, designed by Casson Mann, Sellafield Visitors Centre, Cumbria, United Kingdom, 2002. Typographic transformations designed by Nick Bell. Photograph by Andreas Schmidt.

Casson Mann's 2002 design of the Sparking Reaction exhibition at the Sellafield Visitors' Centre in Cumbria was on the site of a controversial nuclear power plant operated by British Nuclear Fuels Ltd. (BNFL). Part public relations facility and part science museum, the project presented positions for and against the use of nuclear power, explained how nuclear power is generated, and surveyed energy use. The content was developed by the Science Museum of London on the condition that it was given editorial autonomy by BNFL. The project exemplifies how issue-based exhibitions contend with the absence of engaging or provocative artifacts.

Because there were very few artifacts in Sparking Reaction, the design focused upon staging a large amount of textual information in ways that would maintain the interest of visitors. The designers created a central arena called the Core that contained projection screens on the walls and floor with typographic transformations that sequenced arguments for and against nuclear energy. The observer/reader was staged as a figure immersed in words and images with the scale of the projections blurring the relationship between screen and viewer. Just as Lissitzky and other avant-garde designers appropriated photomontage for the purposes of exhibition design, Casson Mann employed the saturated colors, motion graphics, and luminous imagery of contemporary media and advertising.

The status of exhibition design as a form of representation comes to the foreground with particular focus when the topic is architecture. Strategies of display in architecture exhibitions take on a metonymic relationship to the subject: the space of the exhibition presents an opportunity to evoke the spatial and environmental character of the architecture under consideration. Exhibition design can provide a powerful framework for the more conventional—and sometimes less vivid—use of scale models, photographs, and drawings. Two exhibitions about the work of architects—presentations that were also designed by the architects in question—show how exhibition design strategies can represent and embody the spatial and conceptual character of architectural practices.

Barefoot on White-Hot Walls, a 2004 retrospective of Peter Eisenman at Vienna's Museum of Applied Arts (MAK), featured models, drawings, photographs, video, and partial reconstructions of projects. Staged in an immense double-height space, the exhibition was both a representation and an example of Eisenman's theory-driven work. Visitors entered a dark space populated by a series of boxy-volumes—all the same size—set on a regular grid. The space between the boxes was ample, suggesting a pedestrian boulevard through an enigmatic, featureless city. Light seeped into the exhibition hall from reveals at the bases of the boxes and the various slices, doorways, and peepholes. Visitors were drawn to these light-filled spaces, sometimes filled entirely by a model that one could only peer into, other times offering a bench and a video monitor, and sometimes featuring architectural fragments from Eisenman projects. A false ceiling compressed the space of the gallery, but within these smaller volumes the space reached up to the original ceiling, illuminated by skylights. The effect was of a series of austere, modernist "chapels," each devoted to a particular project, a conference proceeding, or an interview. Eisenman's work has always been preoccupied with the grid, and this exhibition heightened this diagrammatic approach by introducing the contrast between the lateral spread of the exhibition space, and the fantastic double-height voids of the chapels.

Without hierarchical cues or predetermined procession, visitors make their own path through the exhibition. The various boxes were sometimes featureless on three sides with a small opening on the last surface. The "fuck you" effect was heightened by the unpredictability of these openings: visitors frequently walked around the box, searching for its opening. Text panels were located near the boxes, but frequently their orientation was at odds with the openings, frustrating viewers who wished to read about the project in proximity to their view of the project. It was a "difficult" exhibition in a way that paralleled the abstruse, aggressively formal character of Eisenman's architecture.

Yet with this lack of hierarchy also came a kind of freedom for the visitor. The grid dispelled the burden of a linear story: all routes through the space were equally valid, and the surprise of encounter was its own reward. The abstraction of the grid fostered a kind of independence for the observer. But this independence could also be alienating for visitors less prepared for—and tolerant of—the demanding subject of theory-driven architecture. Ultimately what was missing from the exhibition—despite its considerable pleasures—was the dimension of editorial or curatorial interpretation. This was not necessarily an effect of the formal attributes of the show, but more a by-product of how the projects were contextualized. Extremely short text panels frustrated attempts to understand the significance of projects within Eisenman's oeuvre. For an architect who places such importance on textual sources, it was a remarkably stripped-down presentation, as if the models and photographs were self-sufficient.

Where observers of the MAK exhibition entered a cerebral and hermetic space—almost liturgical in its tone—a 2006 survey of the work of the Los Angeles-based architecture studio Morphosis at the Centre Pompidou in Paris felt more like a chic nightclub. Visitors to Continuities of the Incomplete were obliged to slip protective booties over their shoes before striding onto a glass ramp. Arrayed under the glass surface were models, photographs, drawings, monitors, and text panels. Skeptical or uninterested visitors were drawn into its space by the seductive glow of white-blue light. The exhibition's "Big Idea" was the transformation of the angle of vision—the shift from wall to floor—and it succeeded in transforming the often prosaic and abstract elements of architectural exhibitions into an engaging, full-body experience.

All architectural exhibitions confront the problem of scale: the Morphosis survey met this dilemma with humor by making the visitor feel like Godzilla in Tokyo. Striding across Los Angeles, peering into little models, visitors were given an omniscient overview of the space, free to wander in and out of projects. Visitors walked over the face of Morphosis founder Thom Mayne as talking-head interviews played from beneath the glass, with his voice projected from above. The bird's-eye view was particularly effective for the work of Morphosis because its spectacular forms—as dense and attenuated as muscles and tendons—are best observed from above. Morphosis's attention to the urban context was well served by the perspective of this exhibition.

Walter Benjamin's classic 1936 text *The Work of Art in the Age of Mechanical Reproduction* discussed the erosion of the "auratic" character of the original art object (which was seen to have an aura) in the modern age. Benjamin saw this process as an inevitable result of the rise of photography and film, expressions of a modern age in which "exhibition value" supersedes the "cult value" of magical and religious art. "Originally the contextual integration of art in tradition found its expression in the cult. We know that the earliest art works originated in the service of a ritual—first the magical, then the religious kind."

Benjamin's term exhibition value is a useful notion in the context of exhibition design: film and photography are, more than ever, the paradigmatic experiential media of our age. Many of the techniques of exhibition designers—from El Lissitzky to Charles and Ray Eames to the present—approximate the immersive character of film. One could argue that exhibition design is an ongoing struggle between the solitary form of the book and the communal form of film. Entertainment media are affecting exhibitions just as surely as they are affecting education, politics and the rest of contemporary culture.

In tracing the shift from art's origins in its cult value to its modern form of exhibition value, Benjamin describes aura as that "which withers in the age of mechanical reproduction." Exhibition design is an agent that works against that withering, using its techniques to reinvest objects and images with the aura that derives from seeing them in unique physical circumstances. What is exhibition design if not an attempt to stage objects and observers in ways that restore the experience of objects and images with what could be called "aura" or "authority" or—less exalted—"relevance"? If, following Benjamin, exhibition value is what surrounds us in contemporary media, then exhibition design represents ways to gain attention in a culture suffused by competing modes of entertainment. The promise of exhibitions is that a face-to-face encounter—with a painting, an object, a physical site—will provide something that cannot be captured otherwise in photographs or reproductions.

First published in *Eye* Vol. 16, No. 61 (Autumn 2006)

1. Silvia Monaco, "Ronan and Erwan Bouroullec: Textile Field," *Domus* blog, October 21, 2011.

Continuities of the Incomplete,
Morphosis survey, Centre
Pompidou, Paris, 2006. Photograph
by Graham Ferrier.

Barefoot on White-Hot Walls,
Peter Eisenman retrospective,
Museum of Applied Arts
(MAK), Vienna, 2004. Photograph
by Wolfgang Woessner,
courtesy of Eisenman Architects.

A GATHERING OF SWANS

From the journal of a Mr. Patrick Conway, aged 17, during the course of a visit to Bruges in the year 1800: "Sat on the stone wall and observed a gathering of swans, an aloof armada, coast around the curves of the canal and merge with the twilight, their feathers floating away over the water like the trailing hems of snowy ball-gowns. I was reminded of beautiful women; I thought of Mlle. de V., and experienced a cold exquisite spasm, a chill, as though I had heard a poem spoken, fine music rendered. A beautiful woman, beautifully elegant, impresses us as art does, changes the weather of our spirit; and that, is that a frivolous matter? I think not."

The intercontinental covey of swans drifting across our pages boasts a pair of cygnets, fledglings of the prettiest promise who may one day lead the flock. However, as is generally conceded, a beautiful girl of twelve or twenty, while she may merit attention, does not deserve admiration. Reserve that laurel for decades hence when, if she has

Spread from Richard Avedon and Truman Capote's *Observations*, designed by Alexey Brodovitch, 1959. The large format of the publication provides expanses of white space, punctuated by initial capitals in Didot.

through thick and thin: fashion and type

Typefaces are abstract. Barring letters that have an overt figurative origin (characters made of branches or rope), the domain of typography and lettering is refreshingly content-free, a matter of style, history and functionality. Yet, as typefaces and lettering are employed in related contexts, the associations of these contexts bleed into our understanding of the typeface itself. Type designer Tobias Frere-Jones once recounted his experience developing a logo for a company that produced hair products, false nails, and perfume. After working to produce an appropriately "feminine" logotype he arrived at a high-contrast sans serif that intuitively felt right. He checked his work against the competition by making a trip to the drugstore and discovered that Almay, L'Oréal, Revlon, CoverGirl, and Maybelline follow an almost uniform typographic code, most sharing the stylistic root of the typeface Optima: he knew the "right" typeface before he realized he knew it. "What is so feminine about Optima?" he asked, as he wondered whether these gendered associations are inherent in the forms of the typeface, or evolve from patterns of use. Such patterns of use can become so pronounced that they shape our understanding of typography.[1]

This phenomenon is observable in the arena of fashion, where serif and sans serif tyefaces have articulated a certain landscape among fashion magazines and fashion brands. Over the twentieth century, carrying into the present, one can observe competing aesthetics of modernity, traceable through different uses of the modern typefaces of Didot and Bodoni and the avant-garde aesthetic of sans serif grotesques.

fashion x-rays

The late eighteenth- and early nineteenth-century typefaces of the Frenchman Firmin Didot and the Italian Giambattista Bodoni are classified as modern because they introduced an extreme contrast between thick and thin elements, achieving a radical consistency among letter shapes by subjecting the variety of the alphabet to a thick/thin autocracy.[2] The result is a abstraction and precision, echoing their Enlightenment origins. Bodoni and Didot exaggerated the height and verticality of the ascenders and descenders of the letterforms, lending the characters an architectural grandeur. Bodoni described the "beauties of type" as "conformity without ambiguity, variety without dissonance, and equality and symmetry without confusion. A second and not minor value

is to be gained from sharpness and definition, neatness, and finish."[3] Bodoni's prescription would be equally at home in a classical treatise on type, or in a 1950s book on proper grooming for debutantes.

Didot and Bodoni dominated printing until the late nineteenth century, when the Arts and Crafts movement returned to the solidity of humanist letterforms and the texture of Renaissance printing (William Morris called Bodoni's letterforms "shatteringly hideous").[4] After fading from view, Bodoni and Didot made a comeback in the early twentieth century, partly because their geometric clarity seemed modern again. An Italian foundry, Nebiolo, issued a new cut of Bodoni in 1901, and ten years later the largest American foundry, American Type Founders, issued its own very popular cut of Bodoni.

In 1912, Deberny & Peignot bought the original punches of Didot, making the font newly accessible to designers. In a classic portrait, Charles Peignot, the head of the French foundry, was photographed with a beautiful poster-scaled Didot *a* hovering in the background. It is from this fashionable context of European modernism in the 1920s and 1930s that America borrowed two of its most influential art directors, Dr. Mehemed Fehmy Agha, who would art direct *Vogue* from 1929 to 1942, and Alexey Brodovitch, who served as art director at *Harper's Bazaar* from 1934 to 1958. Both are credited with having imported a modern approach to layout and photography, as well as a modernist sensibility about type.

Brodovitch had used Didot while working in Paris on *Cahiers d'Art* in the 1920s. In his reign as art director of *Harper's Bazaar*, Didot was the black blade that cut the white space of his layouts. The font became the signature of *Harper's Bazaar* as well as Brodovitch's own signature: he used the font for the identity of his influential Design Laboratory at the New School. In the 1950s, Bodoni (and its clownishly bloated progeny Bodoni Poster) was used in many other design contexts. The cover of a 1950 Museum of Modern Art book, designed by Jack Dunbar, prominently displays its title, *What Is Modern Design?* in Bodoni, as if the question it asks is answered by the typeface, rendered in stark white letters on a black background.

fashionizing fonts

The canonization or the "fashionization" of the Didone style can be observed in the evolution of *Vogue* magazine. In *Vogue*'s early prephotographic covers, illustrators created lettering that worked with the

Didot

style and spirit of their illustrations. This ethic was carried over as *Vogue* made the transition into the photographic era: photographers and designers created ambitiously varied and inventive approaches that integrated letterforms as part of a total approach to design. But even in those covers that did not integrate the lettering as part of the overall concept, type choices were extremely varied.

As late as 1955, *Vogue* covers vacillated between serif and sans serif typefaces, as well as script faces and illustrative, photographic letters. It was after 1955 that the magazine appears to have legislated a consistent use of the all-capitals banner headline set in Didone lettering. Apart from minor details, it has remained absolutely fixed since then, the trade dress of a powerful international franchise.

bazaar aesthetic

Flash ahead to 1992 and the Didone aesthetic is powerfully resuscitated in Fabien Baron's re-design of *Harper's Bazaar*. Baron commissioned Jonathan Hoefler to create a new digital Didot, a kind of super-Didot, drawn in extremely large sizes that allowed the type to be set in enormous display sizes while still retaining its razor-thin lines. When I interviewed Baron in 1995 for *Eye*, he seemed irritated when I asked if his choice of Didot was self-consciously referring to the Brodovitch era: "No...We used Didot because it's very feminine, not because of the magazine's history. When we started at *Bazaar* things were very elegant and the direction of the magazine was about elegance."[5] He applied the same spirit to his advertising and brand work with Valentino and Calvin Klein, and, more recently, his art direction for a book on Balenciaga.

A casual glance through the lexicon of fashion brands confirms that this Didone aesthetic is shorthand for luxury, refinement and a certain posh attitude. To paraphrase Jack Parr's line "Whenever I hear the word culture, I take out my checkbook"—consumers are now trained to take out their checkbooks whenever they see Didot. So why are Bodoni and Didot used so often in relation to fashion, apart from their stylishness and pedigree? Can it be that within the very forms of these typefaces they evoke the precision of tailoring, the flatness of fabric, the dynamics of gathering, draping, and folding? In *Dreaming by the Book*, Elaine Scarry discusses how writers create and manipulate imagery, showing how mental images are subject to bending, folding, and stretching. Typefaces perform similar manipulations, conjuring visual associations, rather than purely mental ones. In my mind, the attenuated forms of Didone letters are not unlike the flattened geometries of dress patterns: accelerated curves and tapered rectangles meeting at precise junctures. One can imagine the fine lines of the Didone serifs as the seams and stitches that connect into an ensemble of parts.

While we can speak of this "imaginary" and associative dimension to Didone fonts, we can also point to one of its most salient, pragmatic aspects: it has an almost see-through quality. Because of its radical thick-thin structure, the mass of the letterforms are greatly diminished: words typeset in Didone fonts act as a typographic veil over photography, making them particularly useful for magazine covers. Like Tom Wolfe's "social x-ray," Didone fonts create an x-ray of the word. Their anorexic, skeletal forms create an ideal overlay for photography. The connection between Didot, Bodoni, and the topic of fashion is so embedded that not only do *Vogue* and *Harper's Bazaar* continue to dress themselves in its sparkling linearity, but so do countless other magazines and brands.

sans serif and chanel

If Didot and Bodoni acquired the unmistakable scent of fashion at this midcentury juncture, the use of sans serif typography in fashion can be connected to a

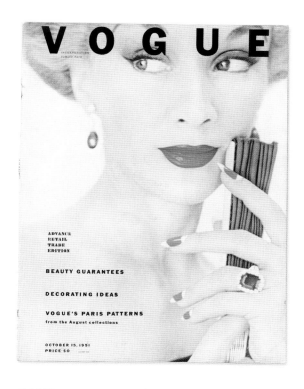

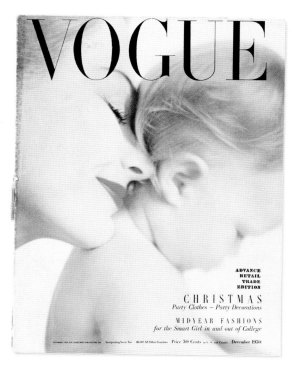

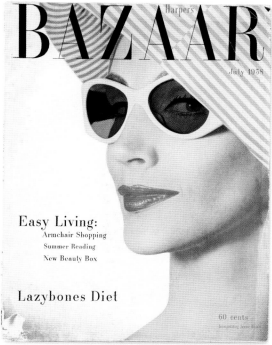

Covers of *Vogue* October 15,
1951 and December 1950;
Cover of *Harper's Bazaar*, July
1958, Art Directors: Alexey
Brodovitch, Jack Dunbar, and
Adrian Condon; Cover of
Harper's Bazaar, March 1993,
Art Director: Fabien Baron

N°5
CHANEL
PARIS

EAU DE PARFUM

Chanel's simple
black-and-white sans
serif label—which
has remained largely
unchanged since
its debut—adorns a
perfume bottle.

Jil Sander logo, designed
by Peter Schmidt,
ca. 1975; Marc Jacobs
logo; Armani logo

The hybrid logotype
of Yves Saint Laurent,
designed by A.M.
Cassandre, 1963.

Yves Saint Laurent
preparing for his 1962
debut. Photograph by
Pierre Boulat.

JIL SANDER

MARC JACOBS

ARMANI

YVESSAINTLAURENT

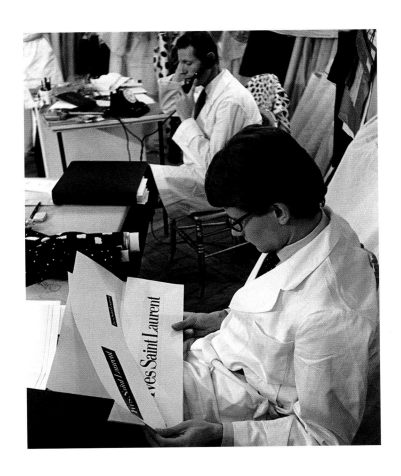

single, powerful instance of design: the brand identity for Chanel. Set in black sans serif capitals against a white field and applied to the cubic apothecary-like bottle of Chanel No. 5 perfume, it aligned itself with the avant-gardism of Le Corbusier and the industrial vernacular. The visual approach (and the mystique of a perfume that was numbered rather than named) was a refutation of the romanticism that dominated women's fashion and perfumes.[6]

The label's little black capitals—like Chanel's "little black dress"—captured the power inherent in understatement. Because it has been part of the commercial landscape for so long, it is hard to see the packaging for Chanel as radical, yet one can retrospectively appreciate its alluring combination of modesty and authority, an effective analogue for Chanel's urbane style. Chanel's sans serif set itself against the cultivated and super-refined aesthetic of Bodoni and Didot, as well as against the loopy and voluptuous scripts used for other perfumes, clothing, and "fancy" goods. We see the same attitude expressed in the sans serif logos for Rei Kawakubo's label, Comme des Garçons, and bold sans serif wordmarks for Jil Sander, Helmut Lang, and Fendi. But the Chanel lettering also carries a vaguely *moderne* quality that has a related but distinct progeny in Givenchy and the contemporary-retro spirit of Marc Jacobs.

the "third position" and yves saint laurent

In 1962, as Yves Saint Laurent was preparing his first collection under his own label, Pierre Boulat photographed the anxious young designer holding two cards: both feature his name set in Didot, one with white type against a black field, the other with black type against white. He must not have been satisfied because the following year he unveiled a new logo commissioned from the poster designer A.M. Cassandre.

The Yves Saint Laurent signature became one of the most distinctive graphic signatures in the world of fashion, and was one of the last pieces Cassandre would produce before his death. If we can think of the sans serif grotesques of Chanel as staking out one aesthetic pole, and the Didone world as another, Cassandre and Yves Saint Laurent claimed a third position—letters that are neither serif nor sans serif, not strictly roman or italic or even a proper script, but a complex hybrid of all of these forms. The YSL logo expresses the ambivalent modernity of Cassandre's last typographic style, reflecting his disappointments with what he saw as

the coarseness of advertising and the declamatory style of poster art that he had pioneered.

With the YSL mark he wanted to create modern letters that also reflected the gestural and rhythmical forms of handwriting. Yet one could argue that with this "third position" between serif and sans serif idioms, Cassandre was also playing with the subtle codes of gender and sexuality in the YSL logo, just as Saint Laurent himself played with the intermingling of masculine and feminine languages in his designs for clothing. Saint Laurent's mystique as a gay man surrounded by beautiful people of both sexes was part of the YSL brand promise, as was made clear in a perfume ad featuring a Jeanloup Sieff portrait of the designer, naked with his legs crossed to obscure his crotch; he was not carnal as much as pansexual, a figure of both male and female sensibilities.

If Chanel's identity exploited the traditionally male (industrial, abstract, mechanical) characteristics of sans serif for a decidedly "butch" logo, and if the forms of Didot and Bodoni were so intricately wed to notions of fashion and femininity (the ultimate "femme" typefaces), then Cassandre's YSL logo could reasonably be considered a "queer" typeface.

First published in *Eye* Vol. 17, No. 65 (Autumn 2007)

1. Tobias Frere-Jones, "Drugstore Travelogue," in *Sex Appeal: The Art of Allure in Graphic and Advertising Design*, ed. Steven Heller (New York: Allworth Press, 2000).

2. My interest is in the broad stylistic characteristics of Bodoni and Didot; there are now more than five hundred versions of Bodoni. See Cees de Jong, Alston W. Purvis, and Friedrich Friedl, *Creative Type* (London: Thames & Hudson, 2005).

3. Alexander Lawson, *Anatomy of a Typeface* (Boston: Godine, 1990), 200.

4. Ibid.

5. Fabien Baron, "Reputations: Fabien Baron," Interview by Abbott Miller, *Eye* vol. 5, no. 18 (Autumn 1995).

6. Kenneth E. Silver, "Flacon and fragrance," *Chanel*, ed. Harold Koda, Andrew Bolton, and Rhonda K. Garelick (New York: Metropolitan Museum of Art, 2005).

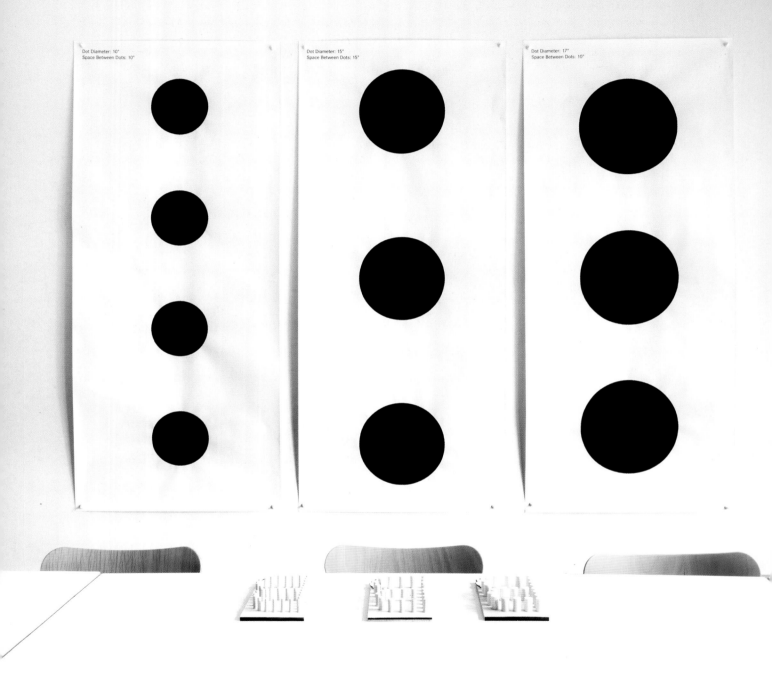

the elephant in the room

The international design firm Pentagram was founded in London in 1972. Over the past forty years different graphic designers, industrial designers, and architects have worked within the unique, multidisciplinary practice. The studio is based on a partnership model, with each designer-partner leading his or her own team of designers. There are frequent opportunities for collaboration, shared knowledge, and shared resources. The original founders of Pentagram established a principle of sharing profit equally among partners, instilling a unique dynamic of responsibility to the larger group. The following discussion with four partners—Michael Bierut, Eddie Opara, Paula Scher, and Abbott Miller—was held in the New York office on March 20, 2013.

ABBOTT When I was considering joining Pentagram, I was anxious about losing some of the particularity of my individual perspective. I'm curious about how each of you negotiated the transition from where you were to what you were coming into.

EDDIE I had similar anxieties when I joined in 2010. Is it more open; are you more open; are you more free? I think it's up to the partner, really. On certain occasions I don't think it's that free, or freewheeling, when you've got a certain target of profitability that you have to hit. You're anxious; there's pressure. But I think that's also beginner's nerves, to a certain degree.

PAULA It has to do with how you come into the group. When I joined in 1991, I was a woman whose business partner had left; I was carrying debt and also doing the same kind of jobs I had been doing for the past seven or eight years. I knew that if I didn't change I would do that same kind of project until I would be too old for it. There was a limited amount of room to move, given the nature of the business in the late eighties and also as a woman. There weren't technological hurdles yet, because nobody was computerized. So the issues were more about how you were going to be perceived. What were the outer expectations of what Pentagram and I, as an individual, could do? The goal was always to cast that net as broadly as possible so that it didn't matter what I could do; it just mattered what people thought I could do. So if someone thinks I'm an identity guru, that's great, and if someone else thinks I design type on buildings, that's great. It just means that I've positioned myself in a way where the potential of what I can do is broad.

The issue of profitability is different. Making a profit is sort of like turning on the lights; it's something that you have to do. It's part of making sure that you're managing things. But there's a difference between making your numbers and managing your career. They're very different issues.

EDDIE Yes, but when we were profitable in my former studio—even though it was a very small amount every year and it would rise a bit each year—it was modest and incremental. Here it is a thing of its own, a larger entity and a greater expectation. It's still an enormous step from when you're a small independent firm to shouldering a much larger overhead and having partners you feel responsible to.

ABBOTT When you are on your own, your failures and successes are private, and if something goes wrong you are not necessarily affecting anyone else.

PAULA Some of that has to do with when you joined. When Michael and I walked in there was a recession and the newer, younger partners were doing better than the older partners. We weren't doing that great. But we were doing better than the partners we had just joined.

MICHAEL That issue of freedom also relates to individuality and anonymity to a certain degree. Unlike the three of you who came into Pentagram from your own studios, I had been working for Massimo and Lella Vignelli for ten years. I witnessed firsthand the limitations of a clearly delineated offering in the design world. People that went there knew exactly what they were getting. If they didn't get that, they'd sort of be mad. And the Vignellis are versatile designers with a wide range, but the work was always produced within the context of their personalities. At the end of that period, when I joined Pentagram, I felt liberated. Not just because I wasn't working for other people—that I wasn't an employee—but also I had entered into a world where people didn't expect a certain attitude or color or typeface. There is something you expect from Pentagram, but it's hard to say exactly what that is.

When I first came in, I was delirious with the openness: I felt like I could use any typeface, any color, do anything I wanted. But then of course you are still obligated to find your own voice in the midst of that, if you're going to be a good, responsible designer. You have to come out with some authentic voice that comes from within you.

Negotiating that voice within the overall context is a thing you can do on days when it's working really well. It's sort of what Pentagram provides—an open field and a little bit of covering fire for you to maneuver. But sometimes it interferes with people understanding you for what you are as a designer. In the long run, the good outweighs the bad.

ABBOTT I never thought of Michael's pluralism—which you see in so many of your projects, like the Yale posters—in relation to your having worked in such a specific vocabulary with the Vignellis. So much of your work is about the plurality of design languages. It's an almost Oedipal response to the Vignelli years.

PAULA That's what makes us all different in our joining experiences, because they are directly related to where you came from. Whatever the thing was that you wanted to overcome led you to be the kind of partner you are. Or if you wanted to stay the way you were, or whatever the situation was. You have the freedom within the group—separate from the financial obligations—to invent yourself, how you want to play that game, which I think is great. I think it's the hardest thing to come to terms with on an individual basis, and the best part of the partnership.

When a partner has their greatest difficulties—even financially—it's somewhat because they haven't defined where they are, who they are within that group in terms of their own business, and how they're going to manage it and run it.

Some of it has to do with financial things but it's as much about the level and scale of the projects you choose to work on. It also has to do with how your voice gets heard on an outward basis.

Some partners are content to be understood only as Pentagram. There is a collectivization that happens that builds a perception that we can do all sorts of things. But because of the collective impression, it's not as predictable as what you might see in an individual designer's portfolio.

EDDIE I'm often asked, what's in the secret sauce? I mean, it's not a McDonald's Big Mac, you know. It really isn't. There is no recipe. You have to define your own recipe, really.

PAULA I think working within Pentagram makes you smarter than being on your own. Sometimes I'll have conversations with people who are alone in their own businesses. And I often find they're interpreting the project in a really narrow way, in terms of understanding the brief and the client's expectations. They haven't had the benefit of the collective wisdom of what's possible.

On an individual level, all of us can imagine a job at Pentagram as a much, much freer place to navigate and develop and make something happen than in other organizations, because their experience is too narrow. They haven't seen somebody else do it right next to them.

ABBOTT At whatever point you come into Pentagram, you're seeing brand new partners, and you're seeing people who are in the middle and later parts of their careers, and some figuring out how and when to leave. You'd never have that perspective—or at least not as intimately—on your own.

MICHAEL You're watching your peers figure it out.

PAULA It's like living with the ghosts of Christmas past and Christmas present.

[laughter]

ABBOTT When Lisa [Strausfeld] joined Pentagram I think we all thought, "finally the 'technology partner' is here." In fact she was not really interested in technology per se, but what visualization and interaction could enable. She identified that attitude as the core of her experience working with Muriel Cooper at MIT—technology is not an end in itself and should not be fetishized.

She confirmed something that many of us already felt on an instinctive level but had not articulated. She reasserted the role of the designer, not as a technologist but as a communicator, someone who is asking fundamental questions about communication and form. That influenced the whole group. It gave us license to think about technology-related issues in a way that brought it right back to design.

EDDIE Sometimes, I'll talk about technology in a more technical way to get the bloody job. Because if you carry on talking in design speak, it only gets you so far. At some point you've got to cut it off and just say, look, we're going to build it on this; we will code it like this; we have to use x, y, z…. You might not know what I'm talking about, but you've come to me because

I know what I'm talking about. And then we don't have to talk about it anymore!

MICHAEL It's like if you're in a meeting with a client and you start talking too much about typefaces, it's a sign that something's gone really wrong...

ABBOTT The worst is when you innocently drop the name of a font in a meeting, and then the name actually becomes an issue and starts to color the perception of the design.

PAULA That's bad: you can never refer to Akzidenz Grotesque! Accidents and grotesque, how can that be good?

MICHAEL Requiem is kind of depressing too!

EDDIE I think this goes back to what language you're comfortable with and what you think the client is comfortable with. You don't have to talk about the tech part of it because it's really about the design, the functionality, and how it can—especially for the web—connect in a social manner and communicate to people.

ABBOTT You take on a bit of the intelligence of the group, which brings some confidence to do new things or step outside yourself.

PAULA But there are limits: I've found there are things I've never done that I don't have any desire to do that I thought I would want to do. I don't care if I ever design an exhibition, and I think it's because an exhibition goes away. I don't like that! I like things that stay around.

ABBOTT That's why we all design books! That's why I wanted to publish this book on my work.

PAULA My record covers from the seventies and eighties are still around. So the notion of the permanence is really important. But environments, I don't know how I know how to do them, but there is something great about the physicality of it, and if it's built, it's going to stay there a while. For me, that becomes exciting. Part of the problem I've had with digital media is that it's so temporary.

ABBOTT It's incredibly temporary. I couldn't include any of the websites we've designed in this book because it just seems odd to see it on paper.

PAULA It's like television. But television is both temporary and permanent at the same time, because it has this repetitive quality to it. The audience sees the same thing at the same time, and you have that hit of recognition, which, of course, may change. Websites are so dispersed.

EDDIE It's the ability to archive. Television is an archivable medium that you can play again and again and again on any type of system. But for something like the web, or things that are based on specific software, you're dependent upon the software company. You're dependent on whether they make it or break it, and whether they go out of business, or if the software gets wiped out, like Adobe Flash. And then everything becomes totally obsolete. I would go out of my mind if I only did technologically based projects day in and day out. That's why I do the books and the brand work, and something like the interactive table we did for Savannah College of Art and Design, where there is a sense of the object.

MICHAEL With everything we do you get two moments of pleasure. One is along the way when you're designing it; if you're lucky, you have this moment where you realize that "this is it," it clicks into place, and you know...

PAULA Like "This could be the best thing I've ever done!"

MICHAEL There's that. But then there's also that moment where, all of a sudden, it's out in the world, and it becomes part of the landscape. It's the pleasure you get when you encounter this thing you did out in the world. It can be incredibly minor, like seeing a book you designed used as a prop in a photo shoot for a magazine: "There's my book!" Or when you go to Poland and you see a Citi ATM and your logo is on it.

PAULA Yes, that is really gratifying. That's why environmental graphics are great: they're big; they last longer. You [Abbott] can walk by Cooper Union any time of the day, and there is your signage! I was with my childhood friends this weekend, and they pointed out every time they saw a Citi logo or a Windows logo.

MICHAEL But that effect you have on people will vary: I was talking to a potential client yesterday and he was saying, "Well, what have you guys done that I would know?" And I said, "Well, we've done Citi, Windows, the Jets, the sign on the New York Times Building, and just redesigned all the parking signs in New York." And he said, "You guys did the Barnes Foundation too, didn't you?" And so different projects resonate differently for different people. Everyone can be in a room while the Super Bowl is on or can walk by the Barnes Foundation, and everyone is consuming the same culture out there. And that's another thing that makes Pentagram distinctive—the clients are genuinely eclectic. I've never heard a partner declare, "My goal is to work only for this kind of client."

ABBOTT We talk a lot internally about the culture of Pentagram. After forty years, there is a lot of culture and mythology handed down through mostly funny stories. The founding partners were giants in their fields. In today's design scene there's less of an appetite for giants, as people work in collaborative teams, and there is so much interest in the user and crowd-sourcing. Sometimes the personal and authorial notion of design can seem of another era.

PAULA I don't know that anybody is truly collaborative. I think there is a generic methodology that is masquerading as collaboration. The fact is that to make something look like something, you can't do it in a broad group. In a broad group you can perfect something, but you can't actually define it or invent it. If you're working with an architect and a lighting designer, you can refer to that as "collaboration." But they are actually individuals with very specific viewpoints who add a layer of their expertise to something.

And that's why when you see work done in collaborative graphic design studios, it's often so unsatisfying. To work seamlessly they have to rely on a methodology that's ultimately going to equalize everything. The work becomes homogenized.

MICHAEL Each of us walks around with our brain in our own skulls, and that's really where ideas come from; that's where creativity comes from. I think partners in Pentagram—by the very fact that they joined—realize that being in a larger group aids that process.

ABBOTT What I am pointing out is that, culturally, we really are a different model than the agency model or the more anonymous, team-based model. Even though we don't talk about it much, I think we all subscribe to a more individualistic attitude that may be more personal or romantic or whatever you want to call it.

PAULA It is deliberate, and it's not a recent development but goes back to the founders. All of the partners are strong individuals. Nobody among us disappears into a room. This understanding of the partners' individuality is what inspires the other partners, what makes us competitive and motivates us to grow. Maybe I am just showing my age, but it seems to me to be a more satisfying position than to be part of this broad team effort. Collaboration means agreement, and agreement means nobody agrees. So you either don't care or you're abdicating a certain amount of your feelings for the group to arrive at a consensus. It's like rounding out the corners and homogenizing the work to make it acceptable to everybody.

ABBOTT One of my clients is the CEO of a successful international company. It's confounding to him that we operate without a CEO or a managing director...

PAULA It's sort of appalling; we have no hierarchy—there is no Mr. Pentagram; there's no higher authority that somebody can appeal to; there's nobody to say to another partner, "You're fired!" There's no way to get everybody to behave in a meeting; that can be very frustrating. Imagine if we were really big?

ABBOTT Well, the way we operate may ensure that we can't be really big.

MICHAEL I have a friend who used to run a big ad agency. He can't figure out how we can keep it going, you know? He keeps thinking that it's got to fail sooner or later because it doesn't have anyone in charge. I'm not sure you can do it both ways. One of the reasons I think collaborative work is so popular is that it's actually a very useful idea to bigger organizations. If you're a large firm, and owned by an ad agency or a media conglomerate, they don't want individual voices. Those "individual voices" can't be fired without jeopardizing the business. What they really want are people that are basically interchangeable.

PAULA Remember that dinner where [the CEO of a large branding agency] said, "Well, all of our designers are interchangeable"? I wanted to punch him in the face.

EDDIE My project manager's father is a businessman, and he has the same questions about a CEO; he said, "You'd make more money."

MICHAEL If someone were put in charge to run the place, they'd look at all the work we do and say, "Why are people doing these jobs that are either for free or that obviously lose money?" And then the partners would say, "Well, this organization is doing amazing things for kids or for the city or for artists, or I can be more creative, or this will get us some nice attention."

Then our new CEO would say, "Fine, but do it on your own time or just do less of it, or there's a limit to how much of it you can do." And then our CEO would start coordinating our schedules to be better able to take on large multinational projects by simply ordering everyone to show up to meetings and do this and do that. And once you are structured that way you can actually convert overnight to doing really huge jobs...

But of course you'd get a lot of attrition because most of us would quit. But that wouldn't hurt either because there are plenty of talented designers out there who want a decent, steady salary.

ABBOTT When it was founded, Pentagram was multidisciplinary: product design, graphic design, and architecture.... Now the partnership includes two architects, one architect/industrial designer, one writer, and fifteen graphic designers.... The presence of graphic designers is clearly disproportionate to the original ratio: what is going on? Is the holistic notion of multidisciplinary practice no longer tenable? Have these fields become too specialized or are clients no longer able to see them as all linked?

PAULA That's a really good, tough question.

ABBOTT That's why I proposed titling this discussion "The Elephant in the Room."

[laughter]

PAULA Well, that's really an elephant.

EDDIE I believe that graphic design, as a medium and as a profession, has changed the most out of all three disciplines, and because of that change, it has expanded over more territories and synthesized more domains. People want to know more about it; they gravitate to it, even though it doesn't have the heroic aspects of architecture.

MICHAEL When I think about graphic design versus product design versus architecture, we have three separate, clearly delineated buckets. Eddie is right: graphic design has gotten very amorphous and

pluralistic, spreading out in a lot of different directions. Meanwhile you could argue that architecture has become even more of a capital *A* profession, less permeable to young practitioners and less inclusive of allied disciplines. Certainly, there are younger architects who have more flexible ideas about what architecture is and how it relates to identity, graphic design, and product design.

But those five founding partners of Pentagram didn't quite go together, even on the day Pentagram was born forty-one years ago. Theo Crosby was a thing unto himself; Ken Grange had a really strong, single-minded practice that he liked doing in context with these other guys, but he still ran it as Kenneth Grange Design.

I think there are ways of opening things up again so that Pentagram has a broader mix of disciplines. But still, graphic designers are really different from these other designers. It's really easy to say, "Design is all one thing," but graphic design is about content. Architecture is not about content, it's about form, and expression and problem solving through form; as graphic designers, we have problems to solve through form too, but the problem is always based in a particular content or message.

PAULA Graphic designers are different: graphic design can move fast so we can do lots of different things. But Pentagram is not designed to be that big, really. I mean, what would we do with a partner who had a big architectural staff in this office? I don't know, maybe that's not true; maybe it would work; maybe we just need a different space to work in.

ABBOTT When Luke [Hayman] joined, a colleague of his said, "Ah, yes, Pentagram, where great designers go to die..."

[silence]

ABBOTT No one has a snappy comeback?

EDDIE It's actually a nice comment, come to think of it...

[laughter]

ABBOTT Why, because they bothered to say, "great"?

[laughter]

MICHAEL There is some sense that once you're in it you stay in it.

PAULA We did!

ABBOTT Yes, so far!

EDDIE I hope to...

ABBOTT But not everyone does stay. Is there a particular personality that thrives here?

PAULA I always use the cape analogy. Frank Lloyd Wright wore a cape, Salvador Dalí wore a cape, Superman wore a cape. You can't be so strong and independent and willful about who you are and what work you do that you are inflexible. You'd be continually trying to force everybody into your behavior.

I cannot imagine Tibor Kalman being a partner in Pentagram: he would have wanted to run it; he would want to tell everybody what they should be doing. There are a lot of personalities like that and that's completely reasonable; I think the Pentagram personality wants to be individualistic enough to command their own work but they don't want to manage their business in a vacuum. But we don't want too much structure; that's why there's no CEO. We don't want anybody to tell us what to do. We want to have the support of the office and our partners, but we'll pick our own typefaces, thank you very much!

MICHAEL Pentagram is predicated on this balance between opposites that is fairly tough to achieve. Which is why there are only nineteen partners as opposed to ninety.

ABBOTT You can't be self-effacing or else you'll just disappear and that won't work; you can't be so strong-minded—as Paula was saying—that you just get frustrated when you can't impose your will on the others.

I joined in 1999 and I remember being in the London office and asking why there had never been a woman partner there and why it did not seem to be a priority. The response was, basically, "That's a New York thing" or "That's an American thing." Forty years after its founding, the London office got its first woman partner, Marina Willer. That seems out of sync with the broader culture, but even more out of sync with design, since it's a fairly inclusive profession.

EDDIE But the most amazing thing is not that Marina is a woman but that she's not English.

[laughter]

PAULA The figurehead of London typography is Margaret Calvert. It's not like there weren't any women practitioners.

EDDIE I suspect that at that moment there was a belief that a female partner was not going to work.

PAULA I don't think it was about the design industry. It had more to do with the partners' social behavior internally and what they were comfortable with as a group.

MICHAEL The thing that surprises me is that design in Britain is unabashedly macho. If you go to a design conference and there is a British designer, people get up and talk about their football teams and use it as a metaphor for their presentation. Whereas if you're a male designer in the United States, you sort of think, well, at least I don't have to pretend I know anything about sports.

[laughter]

EDDIE I have done that lecture! I did it here in America.

MICHAEL And how did it go over?

EDDIE It was wonderful.

MICHAEL Even Angus [Hyland] is like really passionate about, what, Chelsea?

EDDIE Arsenal!

PAULA Remember at the Pentagram 40th Anniversary party in London where Domenic [Lippa] and Tony Brook spent the evening in the bar down the block because their team was playing?

MICHAEL Did you see Abbott going crazy when the Ravens won the Super Bowl?

[laughter]

ABBOTT My sister was dating a West Point graduate and they told me they were going to see the Army-Navy game and I asked, "Who are they playing?" As soon as I said it—and saw their faces—I realized the depth of my ignorance, made worse by trying to feign interest to begin with.

[laughter]

ABBOTT One last volley, regarding students. Eddie mentioned that the proliferation of graphic design is one of the reasons there's a new energy around the field. Everybody among the four of us teaches.

PAULA Wait, did we answer the "where graphic designers go to die" question?

EDDIE They should all die.

[laughter]

ABBOTT Seriously, the question is how do you feel about the future of graphics, since each of us is advocating for the viability and longevity of the profession through our teaching?

EDDIE It came up two days ago in this very office downstairs: another critic where I teach told me the graduates coming out of the program are unemployable.

MICHAEL The students are unemployable?

EDDIE Yale students are unemployable.

ABBOTT Meaning that they don't have the right skills for entering the job market, or that there aren't jobs?

EDDIE Pretty much the former.

MICHAEL It's meant as a critique of Yale.

EDDIE I talked to a lot of graphic designers when we were going through the recession. It was terrible for architects in that period but it wasn't as bad for graphic designers. We could manage ourselves. So the students coming out and getting jobs would take the quickest job placement they got, even if it wasn't the most satisfying or interesting job. But now, because the clouds are clearing, there's this sense, from the point of view of certain graduate students, that the way they're being educated is not correct. But I disagree: there's an unbelievable versatility to Yale students. They are so intelligent.

MICHAEL I understand where that observation is coming from, knowing the Yale program. But a lot of those students are being inculcated with this idea that they're unemployable because they're getting a message that many of the opportunities in graphic design are, in a way, not suitable for them because they aren't critical or intriguing enough. They think they have to "interrogate the nature of communication" instead of just laying out a fucking page.

PAULA But the whole point is that when you design a project you're going to push something forward. They're not doing that, because they're beginning from a negative position where laying out the page is not important enough. I get worried for students when they get trapped in their time of technology. If they don't grow to be an imagemaker or something broader and more versatile, they are trapped as a producer in a more limited way. If you can solve problems in a broad, imaginative way and you're liquid enough to accept the fact that things change, you're going to have a broad career. It's going to be great. As long as you can fulfill the level of working through the internship, apprentice, and junior designer roles, and put up with the necessary nonsense to get started, you gain the credibility to move. But you can really move: I've just seen it. I have students who have done phenomenally well in this industry.

MICHAEL I can't explain why I was just looking over the *Pentagram Profile* book this past weekend, but I remember Abbott being quoted as saying that sometimes, when you work on a project you really are serving the material and just trying to figure out the most responsible way you can serve the problem at hand and the material that you've been given. At the other end of the spectrum, you're an active editor and curator—to use an overused word—and taking a strong hand, not just in the visual form it takes or enabling it to communicate, but to actually shape the message at the front end.

Part of being a graphic designer is about hunting down opportunities all up and down that spectrum—as deep and as wide and as broad as you can—because there are possibilities to do really cool things along all of those levels.

EDDIE One has to also consider that for students there's a larger gamut of work to be had now than there was ten, twenty, thirty years ago. There's more stuff; they have to think about more things and different ways to work.

MICHAEL What's thrilling now if you're a student and you love any aspect of this whole thing, your access to stimulation is so, so immediate by comparison. The opportunities are out there. Your ability to make, and to publish, is vast.

PAULA I think it's a great time to be a designer.

EDDIE It's a really, really good time.

ABBOTT Thanks for ending on an upswing!

biography

Abbott Miller is a designer and writer. His studio Design Writing Research was founded in 1989 and pioneered a practice that merged writing, curating, and designing. In 1999, he became a partner in the New York office of the international design consultancy Pentagram, where he creates identities, exhibitions, publications, digital projects, and environmental graphics, with a focus on art, performance, architecture, and design. He is the author of several books and numerous essays on design, as well as having curated and designed exhibitions on design-related topics. Abbott's work is represented in the collections of the San Francisco Museum of Modern Art; the Cooper-Hewitt, National Design Museum; the Bibliothèque nationale de France; the Corning Museum of Glass; Klingspor-Museum Offenbach; the Denver Art Museum; and the Art Institute of Chicago. His work has been acknowledged with numerous awards, including the International Center of Photography Infinity Award, the Chrysler Award for Innovation in Design, and the Augustus Saint-Gaudens Award from his alma mater, Cooper Union. He is a member of the Alliance Graphique Internationale, and has taught and lectured widely. In 2014 he was awarded the AIGA Medal from the American Institute of Graphic Arts, in recognition of his contribution to design.

bibliography

BOOKS

Lupton, Ellen, and Abbott Miller, eds. *The ABC's of* ▲■●*: The Bauhaus and Design Theory*. New York: Princeton Architectural Press, 1991.

————. *The Bathroom, the Kitchen, and the Aesthetics of Waste: The Process of Elimination*. New York: Princeton Architectural Press, 1992.

————, eds. *Design for a Living World*. New York: Cooper–Hewitt Publications, 2009.

————. *Design Writing Research: Writing on Graphic Design*. New York: Kiosk/Princeton Architectural Press, 1996.

Miller, Abbott. *Dimensional Typography: Case Studies on the Shape of Letters in Virtual Environments*. New York: Princeton Architectural Press, 1996.

————, ed. *Brno Echo: Ornament and Crime from Adolf Loos to Now*. Brno, Czech Republic: Moravian Gallery, 2008.

Miller, Abbott, Ellen Lupton, Julia Reinhard Lupton, and Ellen Paul Denker. *Printed Letters: The Natural History of Typography*. Jersey City, New Jersey: Jersey City Museum, 1992.

Miller, Abbott, Ellen Lupton, and Marion Boulton Stroud, eds. *Swarm*. Philadelphia: Fabric Workshop and Museum, 2005.

Miller, Abbott, Patsy Tarr, and Nancy Dalva. *Dance 2wice*. New York: Phaidon, 2004.

Miller, Abbott, Patsy Tarr, Nancy Dalva, and K.C. Bailey. *Dance Ink*. San Francisco: Chronicle Books, 1997.

ESSAYS

Baron, Fabien. "Reputations: Fabien Baron." Interview by Abbott Miller. *Eye* vol. 5, no. 10 (Autumn 1995): 10–16.

Kalman, Tibor, Abbott Miller, and Karrie Jacobs. "Good History/Bad History." *Print* 45, no. 2 (May/June 1991).

Lupton, Ellen, and Abbott Miller. "American Graphic Design, 1829–1989." In *Graphic Design in America: A Visual Language History*, edited by Mildred Friedman (Minneapolis, Minnesota: Walker Arts Center, 1989), 24–65.

————. "Deconstruction and Graphic Design: History Meets Theory." *Visible Language* 28, no. 4 (October 1994): 346–66.

————. "Hygiene, Cuisine, and the Product World of Early Twentieth-Century America." In *Incorporations: Zone 6*, edited by Jonathan Crary and Sanford Kwinter (New York: Urzone, 1992), 496–513.

————. "Line Art: Andy Warhol and the Commercial Art World of the 1950s." In *Success is a Job in New York: The Early Art and Business of Andy Warhol*, edited by Donna de Salvo (New York: Grey Art Gallery and Study Center, New York University, 1989), 29–43.

Miller, Abbott. "The 1980s: Postmodern, Post-Merger, Post-Script." *Print* 43, no. 6 (November/December 1989): 162–85, 202–6.

————. "Alchemy of Layout." *Eye* vol. 13, no. 51 (Spring 2004): 28–35.

————. "Apocalypse Now and Then: Excavating the 1980s." *Journal of Graphic Design* 7, no. 1 (1989): 4–5.

————. "From Object to Observer." *Eye*, no. 61, vol. 16 (Autumn 2006): 43–50.

————. "The Idea is the Machine." *Eye* vol. 3, no. 10 (Autumn 1993): 58–65.

————. "Massaging the Message: Quentin Fiore." *Eye* vol. 2, no. 8 (Spring 1993): 46–55.

———. "Pictures for Rent." *Eye* vol. 4, no. 14 (Autumn 1994).

———. "Through Thick and Thin: Fashion and Type." *Eye* vol. 17, no. 65 (Autumn 2007): 16–23.

———. "Toddler Modern: The Bauhaus as Elementary School." *Journal of Graphic Design* 6, no. 2 (1988).

———. "Tracking the Elusive Timeline." *Journal of Graphic Design* 6, no. 2 (1988): 7.

———. "USA Today: Learning from Las Vegas." *Print* 44, no. 6 (November/December 1990).

———. "What did you do in the Design Studio today, daddy?" *Eye* no. 22 (Autumn 1996).

———. "Word Art." *Eye* vol. 3, no. 11 (Winter 1993).

CURATED EXHIBITIONS

The ABC's of ▲■●: The Bauhaus and Design Theory. The Herb Lubalin Study Center for Design and Typography, The Cooper Union, New York, April–June 1991.

The Bathroom, the Kitchen, and the Aesthetics of Waste: The Process of Elimination. M.I.T. List Center for Visual Arts, Cambridge, Massachusetts, May–June 1992.

Brno Echo: Ornament and Crime from Adolf Loos to Now. Moravian Gallery, Brno, Czech Republic, June–October 2008.

Design for a Living World. Cooper-Hewitt, National Design Museum, New York, May 2009–January 2010; The Field Museum, Chicago, May–November 2011; Desert Botanical Garden, Phoenix, January–April 2012; and Coral Gables Museum, Miami, July–October 2012.

Printed Letters: The Natural History of Typography. Jersey City Museum, Jersey City, New Jersey, October 1992–March 1993.

Swarm. The Fabric Workshop and Museum, Philadelphia, December 2005–March 2006.

Up Down Across: Elevators, Escalators, and Moving Sidewalks. National Building Museum, Washington D.C., September 2003–April 2004.

FEATURED EXHIBITIONS

Everybody Dance Now: 20 Years of Dancing in Print. AIGA National Design Center, New York, 2009.

Exhibit A: Design/Writing/Research. Artists Space, New York, 1996.

Figuration in Contemporary Design. Art Institute of Chicago, Chicago, 2007–2008. Brick/Book, Andrea Rosen Gallery, New York, 1997.

Subjects and Objects: The Chrysler Award for Innovation in Design. San Francisco Museum of Modern Art, San Francisco, 1995.

Voices and Visions: Designer as Author. Northern Kentucky University, Highland Heights, Kentucky, 1996.

INTERVIEWS, ARTICLES, REVIEWS

Adams, Annemarie. "Waste Not, Want Not: An Exhibition Review." *Winterthur Portfolio* 27, no. 1 (Spring 1992): 75–82.

Codrington, Andrea. "Invasion of the Copy Snatchers." *Eye*, no. 23 (Winter 1996).

Drucker, Johanna. "Graphic Design in America." Review of *Graphic Design in America: A Visual Language History,* by Mildred Friedman. *Artforum* (March 1990).

Ewen, Stuart. "Living by Design." Review of Graphic Design in America, Walker Art Center, Minneapolis, Minnesota. *Art in America* (June 1990).

Fischer, Adam Christopher. "(De)signs of the Times." *Metropolis* (May 1993): 111–12.

Friedman, Alice. "Pipe Dreams: The Kitchen, the Bathroom and the Aesthetics of Waste: A Process of Elimination." *Design Book Review* (Winter/Spring 1995): 29–31.

Hall, Peter. "Poetry in Motion: J. Abbott Miller and Design Writing Research." *I.D.* (January–February 1994): 56.

Kinross, Robin. "Theories of the Material World." Review of *Design Writing Research: Writing on Graphic Design* by Ellen Lupton and Abbott Miller. *Eye* no. 21 (Summer 1996): 81–82.

Lange, Alexandra. "Logo Motives." *New York*, August 28, 2000.

Lippy, Tod. Review of *Design Writing Research: Writing on Graphic Design*, by Ellen Lupton and Abbott Miller. *Print* (June/July 1996): 108–10.

Lupton, Ellen, and Abbott Miller. "J. Abbott Miller and Ellen Lupton." Interview by Shonquis Moreno. *Dwell* (April 2006).

McKee, Elysabeth Yates Burns. Review of *The ABC's of ▲■●: The Bauhaus and Design Theory*, by Ellen Lupton and Abbott Miller. *Design Book Review* (Summer 1992): 61–63.

Miller, Abbott. "The Design of Conversation: Abbott Miller." Interview by Isaac Gertman. *Design Bureau*, no. 1 (July 2010).

———. "Reputations: J. Abbott Miller." Interview by John Walters. *Eye* vol. 12, no. 45 (Autumn 2002): 54–64.

Perlman, Chee. "Cut to Fit: J. Abbott Miller and Geoffrey Beene." *I.D.* (March/April 1995): 64–67.

Pierre, Catherine. "Designing Minds." *Baltimore* (March 1998): 64–67.

Raynor, Vivien. "A Centennial in Typography, Celebrated Amid Potted Palms." Review of Printed Letters: The Natural History of Typography, Jersey City Museum, New Jersey. *New York Times*, January 10, 1993.

Rock, Michael. "The Designer as Author." *Eye* no. 20 (Spring 1996): 44–53.

———. "Thinking Design." *I.D.* (June 1997): 88–89.

Sierman, Gijs. Review of The ABC's of ▲■●: The Bauhaus and Design Theory. *Archis: Architectur, Stedebouw, Beeldende Kunst* (April 1992): 55.

Spiekermann, Erik. "Living for Design: Design Writing Research: Writing on Graphic Design" *Blueprint* (June 1996): 44.

Taylor, Rachel. "The Dancer's Image as a Memento Mori." Review of *Dance 2wice* by Abbott Miller, Patsy Tarr, and Nancy Dalva. *Eye* no. 52 (Summer 2004).

Temin, Christine. "All the Modern Conveniences." Review of The Bathroom, the Kitchen, and the Aesthetics of Waste: The Process of Elimination, List Visual Arts Center, Cambridge, Massachusetts. *Boston Globe*, May 15, 1992.

Temple, Will. Review of The Couch, The Freud Museum, Vienna. *Eye* no. 61 (Autumn 2006).

Twemlow, Alice. "Material Matters." Review of Design for a Living World, Cooper-Hewitt National Design Museum, New York. *The Architect's Newspaper*, June 3, 2009, 23.

I would like to acknowledge the support of my family, friends, teachers, colleagues, clients, collaborators, and current and former members of my team at Design Writing Research and Pentagram. My wife, Ellen Lupton, and my children, Jay and Ruby, are each, in their own ways, a source of inspiration. They surround me with their love, intelligence, talent, humor, and music. My sisters, Roxanne, Julie, Michelle, and Laura, connect me to my parents and our Midwestern origins, as does my friend John Swanson and his family. Jane Rosch has been a source of friendship and support since we first met in 1985. My father-in-law, William Lupton, contractor-philosopher, has enabled renovations to our living spaces that are as much part of my learning as my professional endeavors. Mary Jane Lupton and Ken Baldwin, and Julia Reinhard Lupton and Ken Reinhard bring theory and literature to the family table. Kippy Stroud has been generous every summer for fifteen years in hosting an amazing gathering of friends in Maine. Patsy and Jeff Tarr have given me opportunities to do the most fulfilling projects of my career. Patsy's vision, energy, and commitment have sustained our collaboration for over twenty years.

My current and former partners in the New York office of Pentagram—Michael Bierut, Michael Gericke, Luke Hayman, Natasha Jen, Emily Oberman, Eddie Opara, Paula Scher, Lisa Strausfeld—offer advice, humor, and talent any day of the week you happen to need it. I'd also like to thank partners in other Pentagram offices, including Lorenzo Apicella, Angus Hyland, Domenic Lippa, Justus Oehler, Harry Pearce, John Rushworth, Naresh Ramchandani, William Russell, D. J. Stout, Daniel Weil, and Marina Willer. Colleagues whose work I admire and who have provided counsel and friendship include David Albertson, Jonathan Barnbrook, Matteo Bologna, Paul Carlos, Arthur Cohen, Scott Devendorf, Stephen Doyle, John Fulbrook, Michael Maharam, Charles Nix, Rick Poynor, Patrick Seymour, and John Walters.

Over the years I've had a talented group of people on my team: some stayed for a long time and helped define our work and the character of the studio in significant ways. The early and formative "Sullivan Street" studio included the triumvirate of Paul Carlos, Luke Hayman, and Scott Devendorf; fellow Cooper Union alum James Hicks helped advance the sculptural aspect of many early projects, as did Robert de Saint Phalle and Brian Raby in later years. One of my MICA students, Jeremy Hoffman, started as an intern and worked with me for over ten years, becoming an associate and providing a level of craft and care to everything he was involved with; Kristen Spilman, one of MICA's first graduate students in graphic design, worked with dedication and insight for eight years on exhibitions, identities, and web projects, eventually becoming an associate. Kim Walker is the newest associate on my team and, following in the tradition of Jeremy and Kristen, brings an incredible level of talent and wisdom to our work. This book represents their work and that of the whole team: underneath the resolved and carefully composed spaces, images, and typographic ensembles, there are the hands and minds, hours and passions, of many people.

Good teachers shape their students' lives, and I owe a great deal to Rosemarie Haag Bletter for making modernism so alive to me, to Hans Haacke for the bravery of his example, to Rosalind Krauss for her contribution to theory and narrative, to Niki Logis for giving me a vocabulary to think and speak in three-dimensions, to George Sadek for being scary as hell, and to P. Adams Sitney for introducing me to philosophy, Hitchcock, Gertrude Stein, and experimental film.

I've had the pleasure of working with a number of museum directors on great projects, including Tracy Adler, Max Anderson, Richard Armstrong, Graham Beal, Carmine Branagan, James Cuno, Jenny Dixon, Derek Gillman, Mimi Gates, Claudia Gould, Susan Henshaw-Jones, Katy Kline, Tom Krens, John Lane, Bonnie Pittman, Marek Pokorny, Joe Rosa, Michael Rush, Inge Scholz-Strasser, James Steward, Marion Boulton Stroud, Connie Sullivan, Susan Taylor, James Steward, Adam Weinberg, and Connie Wolf.

Curators are inherently collaborative, and I've had the opportunity to create exhibitions and books with especially gifted collaborators. Donald Albrecht and Ileen Gallagher have been curatorial cohorts of mine over the course of many projects and many years. Other valued curatorial relationships have included Carlos Basualdo, Ian Berry, Andrew Bolton, Lisa Corrin, Judith Dolkart, Matthew Drutt, Lucy Flint-Gohlke, Judith Hoos Fox, Jim Fricke, Mildred Friedman, Corinne Fryhle, Ileen Gallagher, John Hanrahan, K. Michael Hays, Jim Henke, Kristen Jones, Harold Koda, Phyllis Magidson, Lydia Marinelli, Melissa Martens, Tom Mellins, Carol Ockman, Sandra S. Phillips, Mark Rosenthal, Margit Rowell, Dennita Sewell, Kenneth Silver, Nancy Spector, Marta Sylvestrova, and Kohle Yohannan.

A number of friends, clients, and colleagues have influenced my work and career, including Ray Allen,

Kurt Andersen, Pam Asselbergs, Meredith Baber, Joanne Bischmann, Gigi Boam, Robert and Dianne Butters, Anthony Calnek, Steve Cantrell, Dorothy Cosonas, Alice Cunningham, Shannon Delage, Mary Delmonico, Renee Hytry Derrington, Miriam Hinojosa Dieck, Deborah Dietsch, Anne Doran, Sara Elliot, Rolf Fehlbaum, Russel Flinchum, Lise Friedman, Tom Gallagher, Marco Garrido, Anna Cecillia Cantone Guzman, Johanna Halford-MacLeod, Carrie Heinonen, Hank Hines, Hella Jongerius, Hiroko Koyama, Emily King, Ned Kramer, Fred Lazarus, Ralph Lerner, Beth Levy, Jennifer Lippert, Kevin Lippert, Bill McDowell, Amy Todd Middleton, Susan Morris, Ravi Naidoo, Walter Pamminger, Jennifer Cole Philips, Alice Rawsthorne, Aileen Roberts, Gwen Roginsky, Andrea Rosen, Bill Roush, Bill Ruprecht, Eric Sanderson, Kate Schlesinger, Andrea Schwan, Laura Shore, Jean Stein, Ben Watson, Jed Wheeler, Richard Saul Wurman, Richard Yancey, and Peg Zminda.

I owe a special debt of gratitude to a number of photographers whose work forms such an important part of many of our projects, including Josef Astor, Andrew Eccles, Tim Hursley, Joachim Ladefoged, Ben Nicholas, Martin Parr, Joanne Savio, Shoji van Kazumi, Ami Vitale, Paul Warchol, Christian Witkin, Katherine Wolkoff, and finally Jay Zukerkorn, with whom I have collaborated more than any other photographer and from whom I learned the meaning of patience and the sense that there is always another angle.

Architecture has been a passion of mine for many years: creating environmental graphics and other projects has brought me into dialogue with an amazing group of architects, including Liz Diller, Michael Gabellini, Simon Hsu, Ron Krueck, Hitoshi Maehara, Michael Manfredi, Thom Mayne, David Piscuskas, Charles Renfro, Jurgen Riehm, Ric Scofidio, Mark Sexton, Jamie Snead, Billie Tsien, Marion Weiss, Tod Williams and Steve Ziger.

I have valued the opportunity to work with a number of artists in creating projects, including Allora and Calzadilla, Matthew Barney, Barbara Bloom, John Currin, John Kelly, Yoko Ono, Nam June Paik, and Doris Salcedo. And in my work with *Dance Ink* and *2wice*, I've been privileged to work with an array of amazing choreographers and performers, including Karole Armitage, Jonah Bokaer, Merce Cunningham, Molissa Fenley, Tom Gold, Susan Marshall, Mark Morris, Stephen Petronio, Paul Taylor, and Twyla Tharp.

Studio members at Design Writing Research and Pentagram, 1990–2013

Chris Adamick
Ric Aqua
Claudia Bernheim
Roy Brooks
Robin Brunnel
Susan Brzozowski
Scott Buschkuhl
Paul Carlos
Yoon-Young Chai
Meg Chaney
Lillian Cohen
Ellen Culpepper
Robert de Saint-Phalle
Scott Devendorf
Alex Dougherty
Deborah Drodvillo
Colin Dunn
Luke Hayman
James Hicks
Jeremy Hoffman
Steve Hoskins
Tracey Hummer
Eric Karnes
Jesse Kidwell
John Kudos
Jenny Kutnow
Paul Makovsky
Joan McCabe
Christine Moog
Brian Pelsoh
John Porter
Brian Raby
Dina Radeka
Casey Reas
Krista Reeder
Jane Rosch
Clara Scruggs
Hall Smyth
Kristen Spilman
Kirk von Rohr
Richard Turley
Olivier Vinet
Laura Lee Vo
Kim Walker
Andrew Walters
Claudia Warrak
David Williams

This book is dedicated
to my family. Abbott Miller

Published by
Princeton Architectural Press
37 East Seventh Street
New York, New York 10003
Visit our website at www.papress.com.

© 2014 Princeton Architectural Press
All rights reserved
Printed and bound in China
by 1010 Printing International
17 16 15 14 4 3 2 1 First edition

EDITOR
Meredith Baber

DESIGNERS
Abbott Miller and Kim Walker, Pentagram

PREPRESS
Andrea Chlad

Special thanks to: Sara Bader, Nicola Bednarek
Brower, Janet Behning, Megan Carey, Carina Cha,
Barbara Darko, Benjamin English, Russell Fernandez,
Will Foster, Jan Hartman, Jan Haux, Diane Levinson,
Jennifer Lippert, Katharine Myers, Lauren Palmer,
Margaret Rogalski, Jay Sacher, Elana Schlenker, Rob
Shaeffer, Sara Stemen, Andrew Stepanian, Paul Wagner,
and Joseph Weston of Princeton Architectural
Press—Kevin C. Lippert, publisher

Library of Congress Cataloging-in-Publication Data
Miller, J. Abbott.
 Abbott Miller : design and content / Abbott Miller. —
First edition.
  pages cm
 ISBN 978-1-56898-726-2 (hc.)
 1. Miller, J. Abbott—Themes, motives. I. Title.
 NK1535.M48A35 2013
 745.4092—dc23
                         2013010636

PHOTOGRAPHY CREDITS

Iwan Baan: 214

James Biber: 202

©Pierre Boulat / Cosmos: 258, bottom right

Will Brown: 51

©Casson Mann: 250

Yoon-Young Chai: 260

Chuck Choi: 55; 61; 162; 163, bottom; 215–17

Design Photography Inc: 161

Jack Deutsch: 84, bottom

Bilyana Dimitrova: 56–57; 157–59; 174; 228; 229, top

Michaela Dvořáková: 45, top

Maria Ferrari: 6; 101; 140, top

Nancy Froelich: 213

Christopher Gentile: 150

©Higashide Photo Studio: 225–27

Philipp Horak: 44; 49; 184–86; 187, bottom;
188, top; 189

Timothy Hursley: 192–93; 194, top; 195–99; 204;
205, top; 208; 209, bottom

Kit Latham: 36–37

Bruce T. Martin: 178; 180–81

Peter Mauss/ESTO: 42–43; 166–71

Charles Mayer: 39, top

Copyright ©2013 Steven McCarthy and
BIS Publishers, Amsterdam: 244 top left

Scott McDonald©Hedrich Blessing: 222–23

Michael Moran: 40–41; 164

Brian Park: 123

Jordan Provost: 148–49

Brian Raby: 221, top; 224, right

Joanne Savio: 34, top

James Shanks: 11, top; 12; 18; 35; 38; 39, bottom;
46–47; 50; 52–53; 79; 83; 86–87, top; 87, bottom;
88–89; 98–99; 104–5; 112–13; 115, top right, bottom;
124; 127; 130; 141, bottom; 142–47; 155; 172; 188,
bottom; 191; 201, bottom; 219, top; 220; 240, 243–44,
254, 257, 258 top left

Alan Shortall: 59

©Studio Bouroullec & V&A Images, Victoria and
Albert Museum: 246

Jorge Taboada: 236–39

Jeffrey Totaro: 173; 230–35

Jessica Walsh: 109

Paul Warchol: 58; 203; 205, bottom; 206–7; 209, top

Sarah Anne Ward: 152; 175; 211–12

Dan Whipps: 54; 63, bottom right; 64; 68, top right,
bottom; 82, top left; 86, bottom; 107, bottom;
108, left: top, middle, bottom; 114, top; 115, top left;
163, top; 165, top; 179

Stacy Zarin-Goldberg: 125–26; 128–29; 131

Harry Zernike; 116–17; 176–77; 200–1, top

Jay Zukerkorn: 10; 11, bottom; 22; 25, left; 26; 28–29;
30; 48; 60; 63, top left, top right; 65; 66–67; 68,
left; 69, bottom; 70–77; 80; 81, top, and bottom left; 82,
bottom; 90–97; 100; 102–3; 106; 107, top; 110–11;
114, bottom; 132–35; 137–39; 140, bottom; 141, top;
151; 153–54; 160; 229, bottom